SPIRITUAL
BOUNDARIES

A Collection of Essays on Social Justice

BY

QADIR ABDUS-SABUR, PH.D.

ISBN: 979-8-89075-063-1

Contents

Dedication

This book is dedicated to Beverly, my loving wife of fifty-five years, our four children: Sekou, Najah, Inas, and Jason, and our nine grandchildren: Rafiq, Omar, Te'onna, Bre'onna, Icis, Inaaya, Inara, Mawunyo, and Seyiram. I pray that The Almighty will guide and protect them throughout their lives.

Introduction

There is a dangerous plague in the United States of America. A new infection that threatens to destroy our nation. It is an excessive emphasis on extremism. We have become people who have replaced spiritually inspired norms and values with extreme individualistic practices of greed and self-interest. Our founding fathers knew the importance of "In God we trust," but some contemporary citizens only trust in themselves. Their path of selfish and vested interests has brought this country to the brink of moral bankruptcy.

What is needed is a moral and ethical standard: a boundary beyond which neither those on the right" nor those on the "left" will be able to trespass for their individualistic causes. We need a collection of norms, values, and ways of understanding beyond man's ability to establish simply through human reasoning. We have historically displayed that our self-interest which manifests itself through corporate donations and government lobbying, interferes with our equitable social judgment.

The boundary that will help this country should be established by Divine inspiration. I refer to it as a Spiritual Boundary--the title of this volume. As a nation, we can never achieve equity and social justice until we recognize that we must answer to a higher authority for all of our decisions. Time and again, even our best, well-meaning legislators have fallen victim to human frailties.

* * *

The essays in the book were written after Donald J. Trump lost his bid for a second term as President of the United States. They were posted on my blog athttp://drqadir44.medium.com/, and some appeared in our local newspaper, The Farmville Herald.

Trump's term of office was marred by controversy. The Washington Post reported that he made 30,573 false or misleading statements during his four years in office. During his tenure as President, he fanned the flames of racial, ethnic, and religious hatred; he made COVID-19 a political issue rather than one of public health, and he was impeached twice for unseemly conduct as President.

After he lost the 2020 elections, he devised what was known as a "Big Lie": the assertion that the elections were unfair and were 'stolen' from him. This assertion led to the January 6, 2021, insurrection. Consequently, Congress established a committee to investigate the events leading up to this attempt to storm the Nation's Capital. Their investigation recommended that Trump be criminally charged for encouraging this attempted coup.

The essays in this volume were written against this backdrop.

1. Building a New America

The first week of November 2008 was a turning point in my life. President Barack Obama was elected, and I felt a deep desire to move to Washington, DC, to assist him in any way possible. I sensed that his leadership, challenging the socioeconomic norms of America, would face many struggles. Relocating was impossible for me, so I began searching for a way to contribute to the monumental redirection of American society. Eight years later, the pendulum swung in the opposite direction.

Our last four years, with Donald J. Trump as our President, have been marred by the accentuation of racial and ethnic hatred that thoroughly characterized our country's earlier history. I recall reminding the Muslims in attendance at one Friday Prayer that The Almighty reminds us in Qur'an (2:216) that we may not like a situation, but by it, He brings about much good. For Black and Brown people in America, the good has been arduous to see during the past four years.

But as my wife and I listened to President-Elect Joe Biden and Vice President-Elect Kamala Harris address our national challenges and their plans to address them, I once again asked myself, "" What can I do to help?" Their message calling for national unity will probably be an uphill struggle, primarily because almost half of our population actively or tacitly supports racial and ethnic bigotry and hatred. So, what can I do?

Notwithstanding, a little more than half of our nation recognizes our need for a ubiquitous development of a new socioeconomic reality that celebrates diversity with equity and justice for all. Our multicultural citizenry speaks and listens through differing voices reflecting ethnic and sociocultural norms that outsiders may not understand or appreciate.

I believe that our collective future is predicated upon our ability to articulate our commonalities rather than accentuating our differences. So, what can I do? I can speak through the voice of my ethnic and sociocultural experience. I can champion the call for strengthening our shared human desire for equity and justice for all citizens. I can work cooperatively with others of different religious and ethnic experiences for our common good. Rather than fanning the flames of socioeconomic partitioning, I can support those activities that bring us together. Most importantly, I can invite you to do the same.

2. Social Aspects of Mathematics: Abstract Thinking

Considering the economic and political partitioning that plagues our country, one must ask themselves, "What has happened to our inherent understanding of honesty and truth?" Where should these normative values have been learned?

I often tell my students that Mathematics is The Almighty's gift to Humanity for understanding His Creation. Well, you can imagine the stares that I get. "But I hate Math! Math makes no sense to me." And some parents are worse. I tell them that their son or daughter needs to spend more time on math assignments, and they proudly announce to me, "Well, I didn't like math either!" I guess I am supposed to infer from this reply, "Don't expect too much help from me!" Using this experience as a point of departure, I thought that discussing a fundamental aspect of Mathematics and how it influences our lives would be appropriate.

Basic Math Facts

In elementary school, youngsters learn multiplication tables: 4 times 5 equals 20; 9 times 7 equals 63, for example. When I was a young scholar, students had to commit these basic multiplication facts to memory—I am not sure whether or not that is a present-day requirement. Nevertheless, students should be exposed to verbal problems that employ these basic facts. I have found that many youngsters do not like word problems. They argue that they are unable to determine which mathematical operation to perform. "What should I do—add, subtract, multiply, or divide?" However, developing problem-solving skills is an essential aspect of learning.

Sharief had five bags of marbles. Each bag had eight marbles. How many marbles did Sharief have in total? Using verbal problems, students realize that it is unnecessary to empty all five bags of marbles and count them one at a time. A solution to this problem is achievable simply by applying previously learned basic facts. A fundamental mathematical concept known as abstract thinking begins with basic facts and then learning to transfer this knowledge to other situations.

As youngsters mature, they apply previously learned internalized knowledge—basic facts—to new situations. For example, Sharief may have to solve the following problem: "How many doses of vaccine can I transport to Nevada if I have five trucks, each of which can carry 7,500 vials of medicine?"

Sharief does not need to count each vial one by one to determine the total. He has learned to trust his basic internalized knowledge, and consequently, there are 37,500 vials of vaccine. He has learned and internalized basic multiplication principles and can transfer this knowledge and logically predict outcomes based on his prior experiences.

Abstract thinking as adults

As Sharief interacts with others in his circle from youth through adulthood, he gradually internalized Divinely inspired basic facts dictating acceptable moral and ethical behavior. He learned that honesty yields positive results while being caught in a lie result in disapproval or punishment. He knew the family and community responsibility are more precious than selfishness and greed. Concern for others and positive interactions built his self-esteem through positive family and community experiences, while greed and selfishness led to social disapproval, isolation, and avoidance. He learned that others treat him respectfully when he responds in kind. Sharief's socioeconomic circumstances may expose him to challenges in these areas of vital human interaction. But these experiences, over time, help him to discern appropriate behavior in his relationship with others.

Elevating these basic ideas to divine

Just as Sharief was able to transfer basic multiplication facts to his daily employment challenges, so too, he must learn to apply abstractly any divinely inspired moral and ethical behavior in his daily human interactions. As he approaches the autumn of his life, he will look back and see, through his own experiences, the times in which he was able to transfer ideas abstractly to various situations resulting in favorable outcomes.

With average maturity comes a desire for peace in one's life. Sharief will recognize that this desirable condition can only be achieved when divinely inspired, moral, and ethical principles are abstractly applied to all human activities.

So, appreciating the concept of abstract thinking learned through Mathematics, when applied to family and community personal interactions, can lead to a more rewarding life: and, hopefully, "The Big Lie" will not find fertile soil in which to grow.

3. The Steep Path:
Reflections on our Future

This time of year, radio waves are booming with beautiful music: songs that inspire men and women to reflect on their relationship with their Creator. In fact, throughout the year, morally conscious music touches and strengthens one's faith and commitment to family and community.

Inspiring musical selections are celebrated in Christian and Jewish traditions. Rhythm for Muslims is the beautiful recitations of the Qur'an in slow rhythmic tones glorifying The Almighty and reminding man of his interrelated responsibilities to one another. Some do not actively identify with religious faith, yet they enjoy songs that quicken the remembrance of morality, freedom, and justice for all people.

Taken together, these rhythmic expressions touch the souls of Humanity and serve as a reminder of one's responsibilities to a Higher Authority—albeit some may view this authority as a belief in the innate freedom, equity, and justice of one man to another.

If people recognized that peace and harmony in society require that we are responsible to a Higher Authority for our actions, then cooperatively working for equity and justice would not be difficult. Unfortunately, this is not the case. Some work aggressively to oppress others. Their greed and economic and social self-interest challenge the ideals of freedom, equity, and justice for all. Inspirational music does not seem to penetrate their self-declared shell of entitlement.

However, the challenges that America is facing today require that we rethink our need to work cooperatively and recommit to this ideal.

This should not be problematic, especially when we are reminded that Muslims, Jews, and Christians are all descendants of Abraham. Even though there is a tendency to exaggerate differences, one should naturally expect a recognition of moral similarities and a spirit of cooperation between Abrahamic cousins. But those few that seek an advantage continue to justify their superior entitlement. Historically, Americans have seen the results of such behavior by misguided men and women who continue to mislead. The echo of human excellence is not resonating in their souls.

I believe America is at a fork in the road. One path will continue to propel us toward argumentative and legislative gymnastics intended to perpetuate economic and social partitioning.

The second is a steeper one. It invites a response to the rhythm of higher moral consciousness: a consciousness in which freedom, economic and social equity, and legislative justice are the rights of all. In such a nation, every citizen will have the opportunity of developing to their full human potential.

The dawn of a New America is on the horizon. We should take pride in our cooperative efforts as we move center stage of exemplary human behavior. I pray that President-Elect Joe Biden and Vice President-Elect Kamala Harris will lead us up the steep metaphorical path. If they are successful, we may find ourselves in that society described by Dr. Martin Luther King—one in which a man is measured by the content of his character and not the color of his skin.

4. Ebony and Ivory:
Bringing Harmony to our American Life

Ebony and Ivory live together in perfect harmony, side by side, on my piano keyboard. Oh Lord, why don't we?

Just as the lyrics in this recording by Paul McCartney and Stevie Wonder suggest the possibility of racial harmony, so have we reached the juncture of the need for cooperation necessary for our survival. This can be challenging because of the fundamental ideals associated with racial partitioning.

Historically, the conflicts between Black and White have been used to gain social and economic advantage. Their perpetuation was achieved through either erroneous arguments alleging the innate mental superiority of some over others or an explanation of religious dogma, both to accomplish the same end.

Legislative efforts have been thwarted through gerrymandering and enactment of state's rights laws bolstering greed and selfish interest of some while exploiting the rights and social and economic needs of others.

Thus, the subtle effects of racial partitioning remain denied and hidden from our national conversation. So, the question posed in the song lyrics, "…Oh Lord, why don't we," is answered within the context of our American history.

Then came 2020—the year of clear vision. Indifference in the governmental processes led to the election of an overtly racially biased president in 2016. Greed and self-interest led to his impeachment and strict partitioning within the halls of government.

Adding to this political malaise was the Coronavirus Pandemic, in which our current administration adopted a position of denial, and the deteriorating climate of our country was further exacerbated by COVID-19.

Racial inequities, social and economic injustice, and differentiated public law applications became a stark, undeniable reality in this setting. The killing of George Floyd by law enforcement, viewed by millions, sparked a new sensitivity. People of all races, faiths and social and economic statuses became keenly aware of the inherent injustices that define our national experience. We began to see meaningful changes on the horizon.

An awareness of human sensitivities replaced historical motivators. Recognizing that we have a responsibility to a higher authority—although we may see The Absolute through the lenses of our personal experiences—we began to listen to a different rhythm: an arrangement in which all of the metaphorical keys play in harmony.

Participants in nationwide protests were of all racial, ethnic, social, and economic classifications. Monuments and icons of racial division were toppled. Congress even overrode the President's veto to prevent the renaming of public facilities to honor confederate leaders. A new day was dawning.

Given our history, bringing harmony to our future will not be easy—the traditional trappings of greed and selfishness nip at our heels. The key, I believe, is to focus on our higher expectations of one another. Identify and accent our human commonalities and work cooperatively for their enhancement. National harmony is possible, and we are witnessing a daily change in that direction.

5. A Spider's Web

After growing up in the hustle and bustle of a big city, I have learned to appreciate a quiet retirement life on our family farm. With more free time, I can contemplate the wonders of creation and its thought-provoking power.

One day, while sitting on my porch listening to the grass grow, I started thinking of the role of public education as I observed a spider approaching an insect trapped in its web. As I watched, I recalled that one aim of education was to transfer the belief, values, norms, and ways of understanding from the elders of a society to its youth. Just as this insect was caught, so too could youngsters become caught in an education web that can produce a beneficial or detrimental result to the child's development.

Many families cling to a metaphorical spider's house and send their children to schools without thoughtful consideration of the consequences. In some cases, this choice proves fruitful: youngsters thrive and grow to become contributors to society. In other cases, the result is problematic.

Education research reveals a plethora of inconsistencies in the education of white and non-white students. For example, people of color are disproportionately more likely to be placed in lower-performing or special education classes. They are more likely to drop out of school before graduation and more likely never to complete a college degree program.

Typically, schools in affluent neighborhoods have larger budgets resulting in more dollars per student to spend on pedagogical and human resources. These additional funds predictably lead to tremendous success in higher education institutions, frequently leading to a more lucrative career and standard of living. Historically, being caught in an education web may provide opportunities for some families, but indeed it is a trap for others.

Unfortunately, many families are unaware of the subtle negative influences on their child's education experience. At some schools, students spend twelve years absorbing notions and concepts perpetuating greed, excessive individualism, selfish self-interest, sexual promiscuity, and religious skepticism through its overt and hidden curriculum. Some schools perpetuate these ideals without the conscious knowledge and awareness of administrators and teachers.

These characteristics result in student underachievement, which then leads to racial, social, economic, and political partitioning in our nation. However, some schools and classroom teachers have helped students develop an internal strength to overcome these negative, subtle influences. Yet, since most school divisions follow a scripted approach to education, well-meaning educators are unable to affect change internally.

So, what needs to be done? Our success as a nation requires us to answer to a Higher Calling than our self-interest. Most people are honest, trustworthy, respectful, and socially responsible. Societal problems manifest themselves when persons do not have these basic sacred values and are in positions to influence legislation and public policy.

Our future education efforts should reinforce the sacred norms and values mentioned above. Once this is achieved and legislators are sensitive to the needs of all students, America will be at the dawn of a new day. New legislation and public policy will produce a practical approach to schooling that benefits all youngsters. When students enter the metaphorical spider's web at that time, they will be on a path to freedom and justice for all

.

6. Establishing Responsible Leadership: A lesson from Jack and Jill Metaphor

There is a classic nursery rhyme called Jack and Jill. You probably recall that "Jack and Jill went up the hill to fetch a pail of water. Jack fell and broke his crown, and Jill came tumbling after."

This rhythmic nursery rhyme we learned as children can be used as a metaphor to explain conditions that influence events in society. Let us assume, for example, that Jack represents leadership in society. Leadership can be of almost any variety, government, education, racial or economic stratification, etc. Jill, then could represent a body of people led by Jack. The couple ascending the hill could then express the desire of this group of people to achieve success and prominence in their shared community life.

Since water is the source of all life, we can relate it to basic human qualities such as honesty, truthfulness, respect for self and others, and shared responsibility. So, climbing a hill to fetch water suggests the challenges one faces in attempting to achieve a meaningful, productive life.

My mantra is, *"Humanity's utopian society can only be achieved when the basic human qualities of honesty, truthfulness, and respect for self and others are guiding parameters."*

In this metaphor, climbing a hill to fetch water may be viewed as the desire to achieve the best possible human existence. For total human development, the best possible existence for Humanity would be in one's ability to achieve satisfaction in their physical/material life, mental/intellectual life, and spiritual life.

If water represents the key component necessary for the continued growth and progress of any society, the members must be honest, trustworthy, respectful to others, and recognize their shared social responsibilities.

Jack fell and broke his crown, suggesting that his leadership, without basic human characteristics, was insufficient to perpetuate the success and progress of society. Society failed without honesty, morality, equality, and justice for all—and Jill came tumbling after.

As we examine our society today, we see morality, justice, and equity being replaced by greed and self-interest. Society suffers when moral responsibility, justice, and equity are no longer the underpinning components of leadership's values. One only has to search the history of the rise and fall of great civilizations to understand the predictability of the Jack and Jill metaphor.

This simple story gives us insight into the problem we are facing as a nation. Dishonesty has led to the January 6, 2021, insurrection in our nation's capital. It manifests itself in our political leader's willingness to support this failed attempt to overthrow the government for personal gain. It is also exemplified in our national conversation, justifying social and economic partitioning.

But there is new leadership on the horizon. Leadership that appears to be grounded in truth, equity, and justice for all Americans. Herein lies our hope. Perhaps we will see Jack and Jill successfully fetch a pail of water within the next four years. Are we at the dawn of a new America with freedom and justice for all?

7. Interfaith Dimensions of Social Justice: One Nation Under God

Considering the racial, social, and economic divisions that accent our country's history, our minds are challenged to answer the question, "Is it possible to truly become One Nation Under God?" The insurrection instigated by our former President thwarts aggressive efforts by Joe Biden and Kamala Harris to advance a legislative agenda that could enrich the lives of all Americans. Political partitioning makes facing the challenges of Covid-19, systemic racial, social, and economic injustices, as well as environmental catastrophes problematic without our understanding and willingness to cooperate as "One Nation Under God."

American history is splattered with the intentions of one group to oppress another: Men against women, Whites against Native Americans, Asians, and other people of color, as well as the ubiquitous tension between various faith groups. Historically the division of power has been maintained politically. But when we assert "One Nation Under God," I believe that we are invoking Divine intervention—we are asking The Almighty to intercede.

Most Americans align their beliefs with one of these traditions: Judaism, Christianity, or Islam, known as the Abrahamic Faiths. They all identify with the prophet Abraham and are descendants of his two sons, Isaac and Ismail. Within American culture, the children of brothers are first cousins, which in this case means that Jews, Christians, and Muslims are cousins. Although there are differences in rituals of worship, there are many commonalities in terms of just and fair treatment of fellow human beings guided by Divine law.

It is not uncommon to find support for differing political parties within a family. One cousin may be a Democrat and another Republican. Similar individual preferences can be found among siblings and even husbands and wives. But it is a scarce situation when one allows their political view to destroy family unity. A healthy family works cooperatively for the good of its members. All members want to be treated with respect. They desire peace in their minds and hearts, physical and material security, and good health. Recognizing these needs, the family works cooperatively to establish an environment where such conditions can be internalized.

Our nation, when viewed as a multi-ethnic family, shares common concerns, too. We want equity and justice for all and an equal opportunity to develop one's full human potential free of encumbrances associated with racial and political power. If we see ourselves as "One Nation Under God," the concerns of each citizen are also concerns of us all, and they are consistent with Divine decree. A nation whose organizational structure is aligned with Divine pronouncements treats all citizens equitably, justly, and with human dignity. There is no place for greed and self-interest at the expense of others in such a society.

The challenges that we face are much larger than political interest. They are challenges to human rights, human dignity, equity, and justice for all. Our American history suggests that we have not succeeded in achieving these goals through perpetuating racial, social, and economic partitioning. Let us now work cooperatively to establish equity and social justice for all by invoking Divine intervention.

8. Pendulum of Power:
Striving Towards Social Justice

Consider a simple pendulum: a weight on the end of a string, and the string is suspended from above. If it is moved in either direction and released, the natural force of gravity causes it to move in the opposite direction. It continues to move back and forth until it slows down and eventually stops—it has reached its state of equilibrium and rests.

The physical phenomenon observable in this simple pendulum can metaphorically describe the power relationships in society. If the weight represented the collective population, then the movements right and left suggest two opposing economic and social ideological perspectives. Supporters of both points of view would like to maintain influence and control over society.

The total influence of one group over the other cannot be maintained indefinitely. A natural force intervenes to change this imbalance—the gravitational force in this example. The movement, right and then left, slows and eventually stops because gravity constantly pulls the movement toward a state of equilibrium; rest and peace.

Gravity is a natural force in creation. So, let's think of this scenario as creation's intervention, or Divine intervention, into an inequitable or unjust social condition.

When one group of people seeks to oppress the human potential of another, The Creator intervenes.

Historically in America, some whites exploited labor to acquire and maintain social and economic power. Blacks' inequitable, inhuman, and unjust treatment were of no concern to slaveholders; laws and legislative agendas upheld this imbalance.

As time passed, the Creator intervened. The inherent human quality of equity and justice brought about substantial legislative change. Today we can see the manifestation of this pendulum movement toward equilibrium through the election of the descendants of enslaved people to the highest offices in America.

But the process itself was long and arduous. The exploration of Blacks gave rise to the Emancipation Proclamation—a movement toward equilibrium. This, in turn, spawned white supremacy efforts through segregation counterbalanced by the Supreme Court's Brown vs. Board of

Education decision in 1954. Notwithstanding this legislation, de facto segregation continued and precipitated the Civil Rights Act of 1964.

In today's highly politically partitioned society, the pendulum still swings. Albeit more subtly, systematic disenfranchisement through gerrymandering, inequity in criminal justice, and discrimination in allocating healthy family resources are in constant motion; those who have, want more, even at the expense of the health and well-being of others.

Just as gravity prevents the pendulum from remaining imbalanced, so does The Almighty prevent the continued oppression of any of His creatures. He pricks the consciousness in divinely inspired individuals and guides them to work cooperatively to correct human inequities. A country at peace can only be achieved when we are guided by The Divine and work cooperatively toward social justice.

9. Plane of Truth:
Geometry of Social Justice

There are three basic elements in Geometry from which all theorems and postulates are derived. They are points, lines, and planes. A point has no dimensions. It has no length, width, or height, yet it exists as a concept required to understand other ideas and concepts. We can think of a point as the primary element of all existence in Euclidian space. In the context of this discussion, a point could metaphorically represent a unique principle, idea, concept, or point of view upon which all else exists within a society.

Two points determine a line. It can be extended indefinitely in either of two directions, each of which can be extended to extremes. For example, a line consisting of an extremely liberal viewpoint on the left and an excessive, greedy/self-interest point of view on the right could metaphorically represent a society constantly struggling to maintain stability.

In a societal context, all decisions must fall somewhere along the continuum of the line passing through these points of view. Legislation is passed favoring one perspective over the other. In time, the power shifts, and new laws are adopted that support the opposing sensitivities. In such a society, there is a constant struggle between two opposing vantage points for control, power, and influence.

Before discussing a plane, let us examine the line metaphor more closely. Consider a husband and wife, each of whom enters a marriage with their own ideas of individual rights and responsibilities. They frequently argue, and family decisions are based on the winner. This, of course, is short-lived. When the disputed topic is addressed again, the results may or may not be the same. Predictably, if neither is willing to change their point of view, divorce is the probable outcome.

Three non-collinear points determine a plane. It has two dimensions: length and width, and thus metaphorically represents a society in which decisions must satisfy all three different ideas, concepts, or principles simultaneously.

The third point in our metaphorical plane is defined as a compromise between the two existing perspectives. Ideas on the right and left must acknowledge and respect the rights of those of the opposing viewpoint. These are the equitable and just human responsibilities defined by The Absolute, The Governor of Creation. So, this creates a Plane of Truth—an environment in which individual ideals, norms, and values are tempered by Divine decree.

A line allows for constant tension between opposing perspectives, but a plane does not. Instead, it represents the environment in which all three outlooks must be satisfied.

In our marriage example, the family is successful if and only if they can establish a point of compromise. Unfortunately, some couples are unable to reach this point and end in divorce. Sometimes, the man and woman must go through several failed marriages before they learn this basic lesson.

Three points can establish balance. For example, a tripod is stable on uneven ground. I believe our Founding Fathers recognized this natural relationship when our government was established with three branches. The legislative and executive branches sometimes support opposing points of view, and the judicial provides the voice of final authority if a compromise is not achievable.

Let us now consider this analogy in the context of our current political situation. Ideas on the right and left have gone to extremes. Each is more concerned with its own interests and blames the other for rigidity.

The stabilizing aspect of the government of our Founding Fathers was the acknowledgment that all human actions were answerable to a Higher Authority— "One Nation Under God."

Today the rigid support of extreme liberalism (do anything you want) and extreme conservatism (greed and self-interest) is destroying our ability to establish a point of Divinely-inspired compromise for the good of us all. We cannot re-establish an environment that celebrates the merit of opposing points of view but yet can yield for the good of us all. I believe a plan of truth is a good plan for our nation's future.

10. Fasting:
Strengthening Social Justice Sensitivities

A common characteristic among people of Abrahamic faiths is the practice of fasting[i]. Our Creator reminds us, "Fasting was prescribed for you as it was prescribed for those before you, so that you may learn self-restraint and God-Consciousness" (Qur'an 2:183). Those of the Jewish tradition celebrate Yom Kippur. Christians practice fasting on Ash Wednesday, Good Friday, and during the days of Lent, and Muslims observe fasting during the month of Ramadan.

The fast duration varies from one day to as many as forty among these faith groups. Although each particular procedure is slightly different; the desired outcome is collectively consistent. Learning to control physical appetites helps one to focus on concerns outside of themselves. Foregoing physical satisfaction vaults one to the awareness of higher concern. Our Creator asks that we fast, and in so doing, we please Him. So, fasting helps us learn self-control and strengthens our God-Consciousness.

Examining our American societal experiences reveals a ubiquitous presence of overindulgence and unbounded appetites. Overindulgence in food and drink plagues us with obesity and serious medical maladies. The greed and desires of influential people force those less affluent families to sustain a more prominent than equitable share of our collective financial burden. While racism and bigotry threaten our democracy and perpetuate social and economic partitioning, these cultural illnesses are exacerbated by individuals whose appetites in this societal domain are unbridled.

Abstaining from food and drink during the period of the fast yields several positive consequences. We learn the power of our minds over our bodies. We strengthen our individual willpower to control when we eat or drink. Meals are no longer under the jurisdiction of our physical appetites. Finally, since fasting is a practice associated with worship, our fast accentuates our desire to please our Creator, and we become more God-Conscious.

Although the societal characteristics mentioned above cannot be added or removed from a dinner plate, it still may be possible to limit their influence on our lives. If each of us were to call upon our innate sense of fairness and just treatment of others, the self-restraint goal of fasting could be met.

The unconstrained desire for power, greed, racism, and bigotry are maladies that effectively prevent the attainment of "Freedom and Justice for all."

Collectively we must learn to control these ubiquitous, anti-societal practices; those in power must learn to share control with others for the benefit of us all. The champions of racism and bigotry must relinquish their support for social and economic partitioning as an instrument of oppression.

These and many other inspiring lessons could be internalized from participation in a Fast of the Abrahamic Faiths, which could help strengthen one's social justice sensitivities.

11. From Many, One: Towards Equity for All

John Adams, Benjamin Franklin, and Thomas Jefferson proposed that the Latin Phrase *"E Pluribus Unum"* be embossed on the seal of The United States of America in 1776. Adopted by Congress in 1782, the motto was originally intended to reflect the unity of the original 13 states. Instead, today it reflects a national concern—the need to unite as one nation of people for the good of all citizens.

Throughout the past two hundred forty-five years, our nation has had cause to revisit this declaration in several contextual meanings. First, international migration has resulted in myriad racial, ethnic, and religious variations in our population.

E Pluribus Unum, in this context, speaks to the process of positive enculturation and multiculturalism.

However well-intended, this Latin phrase has faced severe challenges. They are among those that interpret "from many to one" mean's that the "many" people who participate in our culture must conform to the "one" understanding of mores and values. They support ideals of racial, ethnic, and social intolerance. They vie for power in our democracy and seek to influence legislative policy.

Historically, their efforts have led to the racial, ethnic, social, and economic subjugation of millions of Americans. Their greed and quest for power have metaphorically placed their knees on the necks of poor and working-class Americans. Moreover, their narrow-minded understanding of "From many to one" for all Americans has resulted in an exacerbated racism and bigotry, resulting in economic and social partitioning, ostensibly so during the last Presidential administration.

Similarly, among the Abrahamic Faith groups, differences in worship practices have superseded the myriad of commonalities. So today, we are thoroughly divided. But all is not lost.

In 1956 Congress adopted a new National Motto, "In God We Trust!" At the height of the Cold War and at a time when Communism's secularist ideals were gaining worldwide support, American legislators embraced the need to put Faith in God above all else.

Our Creator has said, "Let there be a group among you who call one another to goodness, encourage what is right, and forbid what is evil—it is they who will be successful" (Qur'an 3:104).

So, if we cooperatively and collectively live by our National Motto, "In God We Trust," the efforts of those intolerant and divisive individuals will not prevail. A significant challenge looms before us, and we must face it together. We can see the pendulum of change swinging from domination toward social justice. These changes, initiated by our recently elected Executive leadership, are moving our nation's moral compass toward equity for all.

12. Ignorance:
Enemy of Social Justice

Freedom, justice, and equality; wisdom, knowledge, understanding, money, good homes, and friendship in all walks of life; peace, love, and happiness. Those of us who were early Muslim converts in North America knew these lifelong goals as "The Twelve Gates to Heaven." Viewed in the context of a healthy multi-ethnic/ racial and religious community, these twelve socio-economic conditions are the desire of all Americans. Yet, what prevents most of our countrymen from achieving this euphoric state? Ignorance!

This essay briefly examines how the deprivation of educational opportunities has undermined social justice initiatives. Then, it looks more closely at primary education's role in preparing students for full participation in society. This brief analysis is followed by a discussion of the inherent potential merits of President Biden's American Families Plan in addressing the social and economic malaise that plagues our country.

Historically there has been a struggle for social and economic control in America. White male landowner domination permeated the struggles of women, Native Americans, Hispanics, Asian and African Americans. Their objective was to maintain social and economic control while keeping others subjugated under their power. Their primary tool for supporting social and economic control was education.

During our colonial period, a woman's place was said to be in the home. Very few received or even had the desire to achieve formal academic training. Men maintained power by perpetuating their perceived superiority and denying women the right to vote.

Education access for African Americans was denied by law. An undeniable historical fact, as well as that of Native Americans, strictly controlled through Boarding Schools.

Either by limiting or denying some people access to public schools or ensuring that the curriculum upheld the social and economic norms and values of those in power, ignorance of marginalized citizens was maintained, and inequity of social justice was successfully perpetuated.

To advance social justice, ignorance of the importance of education must be thoroughly understood. A look at primary education can serve as a motivator for that discussion.

Primary Education

Seven is a significant number in the affairs of humans. There are seven days a week. There are also several references to the number seven in Scripture. For example, the Opening Chapter of the Qur'an has seven verses. Seven seals are mentioned in the Book of Revelations, and the world was created in seven days. So, from a pedagogical perspective, seven could also be a metaphorical representation of the levels of primary education—mastering the foundations of academic learning (primary education) is approximately a seven-year process.

Not long ago, students attended elementary school from kindergarten through 6th grade and then proceeded to Junior and Senior High School. In the seventh grade, students were expected to apply their basic knowledge and skills in new ways. For example, using acquired reading skills to learn about other civilizations in history, their mathematical skills to solve real-world problems, and their writing skills to express new ideas and their opinions. Today, the application of knowledge previously acquired is still an essential component of a seventh-grade curriculum.

Examining this pedagogical process more closely, we realize that students develop mastery in two primary areas in public education: how to read and how to figure. Reading begins with letter recognition, then forming words into sentences, and finally, sentences into paragraphs that express facts and ideas found in history, social studies, science, etc.

Similarly, in Mathematics, students learn one-to-one correspondence; for example, three objects can be represented by the numeral "3." Basic computations can be performed using these numerals to describe these objects' addition, subtraction, multiplication, and division into groups of different sizes.

Once this foundational (elementary) education is complete, students then learn to apply what they have learned abstractly, using their intellect to understand both the physical world and social interactions. This level of skill is usually developed by seventh grade. For example, youngsters can read Science, Social Studies, and History at this academic level and manipulate and understand basic algebraic concepts. Further, they are at an age where they can apply what they are learning in the context of their lived experiences.

So historically, we have seen that ensuring the ignorance of a subjugated population perpetuates some people's political power and influence over those marginalized individuals. Even when a curriculum allows for the intellectual development of all citizens, barriers, such as eliminating preschool programs and increasing post-secondary tuition, are legislated to limit equitable access to further education. A plan to advance equity in education is needed.

A Plan with Potential

The prerequisite for success in primary school is that a youngster is ready to learn. However, social and economic circumstances may prevent students from acquiring the preliminary cognitive skills to scaffold learning. President Joe Biden's American Families Plan offers an approach that may provide adequate support.

The plan offers several initiatives for previously deprived young people. Two which apply to this discussion are free Pre-K for 3- and 4-year-old youngsters and free tuition for 2-year community college students.

The Pre-K initiative would provide youngsters an opportunity to enter a k-12 school prepared to advance to their full potential. In addition, this effort helps to ensure that our children are ready to move into post-primary education during their seventh year as they advance toward their full potential.

The free tuition program insures that qualified and motivated k-12 graduates have an opportunity to achieve academic goals rather than face the restrictions posed by overwhelming financial indebtedness.

This foresightful plan offers a way to advance equity and social justice by lowering the stigma associated with education ignorance. Let us support and encourage others to support the passing of President Biden's American Families Plan.

13. Measure of a Man: Quest for Equity

Booker T. Washington once said, "Success is to be measured not so much by the position that one has reached in life as by the obstacles which he has overcome". This simple statement reflects the experiences of an individual, and it can also speak metaphorically to the challenges faced by a group of people.

I attended a public high school in a large city in the early 1960s. It was a typical urban school with low expectations for students of color and less rigorous academic content. I vividly recall several incidents which have left indelible impressions on my life. After our teacher returned a History test, I noticed that a White friend and I received different grades for the same one-word answers. I asked our White teacher why he had received an "A" and I had received an "A minus?" What mistakes had I made? She immediately informed me, "Your first mistake was being born!"

On another occasion, after completing a career aptitude assessment, I was told, "Tell your mother not to waste any money sending you to college." Notwithstanding, I started college. Unfortunately, because of my poor college preparation, I was required to take all of the remedial classes offered to incoming Freshmen.

I recall once spending all night writing and rewriting a paper. I submitted it, and when it was returned to me, the enormity of errors (identified in red ink) resembled blood from an open wound all over the sheets of onion skin paper. Predictably I did poorly. I was unprepared for the level of academic rigor necessary for university success. After a year, I was dismissed and joined the U. S. Marine Corps.

One night, we were under enemy attack. Incoming rockets exploded all around us, but none hit my bunker. That night I realized that The Almighty alone was my only Protector. He alone decides the success or failure of all human efforts.

After my earlier discriminatory experiences in public school, I wanted to return to college. The Marine Corps had taught me never to give up, and I was determined to defeat the discriminatory underpinning of American society that I had experienced. So, I wrote to the Dean of my former university explaining that I was now a mature non-commissioned officer serving our country in Vietnam and wanted to pursue my education seriously.

I received his reply while I was still in that war-torn country dodging incoming rocket attacks. I sat in a bunker and read his response. He said he had reviewed my previous academic records and saw no indication that I would do any better if given another opportunity. So, he denied me re-admission.

After I was discharged, I was finally admitted to a local two-year technical school. With the support of my wife, my VA Education benefits and a part-time job I began climbing toward social equity. However, with the regular task of earning a living and raising a family, it took me fifteen years to earn a Bachelor's Degree and another thirty-four to achieve the status of Doctor of Philosophy in Social Foundations of Education.

Although the names, locations, and particulars may differ, many Americans faced with systemic discrimination have overcome a myriad of challenges in their lives, too. And if one considers the challenges faced by racial and ethnic minorities in this country, the metaphor also rings true.

But today's America is beginning to ascend the hill of social justice. Our recently elected President and Vice-President are leading our nation in its efforts to face old discriminatory practices that have led to difficulties in the lives of individuals and racial and ethnic communities. The new America will be measured by the depths of racism and discrimination from which it was able to climb.

14. Dusk or Dawn:
Retarding or Advancing Social Justice

As spring turns to summer, a noticeable characteristic is an increase in the length of daylight. New life is visible throughout the country with longer hours of exposure and seasonal rains. Vegetation takes on new growth, and bright-colored flowers come into full bloom. These changes are also visible in man's hearts, minds, and souls.

There are several references to the sun in Scripture. For example, in Psalm 113:3, we find, "From the rising of the sun to its setting, the name of the Lord is to be praised!" This verse associates the sun with the glorification of the Almighty.

In Qur'an, we find that The Almighty says He "is the light of the Heavens and Earth." In that we can see during daylight, we can think of the sun as Guidance from The Almighty. By extending this metaphor, we can think of night as the absence of Divine Guidance.

The sun's light is not visible at night, although the moon and stars reflect it. Extending our metaphors further, these heavenly bodies suggest entities, individuals, and institutions that can reflect Divine guidance even at times when clear direction is not apparent.

Let's think of day and night in the context of our shared experiences. During sunlight members of a society are aware of their responsibilities to one another and their Creator. The challenge facing us is to understand and apply this metaphorical interpretation in our lives to advance equity for all.

Historically our nation has enjoyed sunny days. Legislators, conscious of their responsibility to support equity for all citizens, amended the Constitution to abolish slavery, eliminated states' ability to restrict African Americans' rights, and protected women's voting rights. These are examples of Divinely inspired social justice initiatives.

However, all days have not been sunny. Instead, we have seen great darkness—the absence of Divine Inspiration: slavery, Jim Crow segregation, social and economic discrimination, voting disenfranchisement, and an accelerated reappearance of overt white supremacy, for example. These represent periods of darkness in our history.

But within this darkness, some individuals and institutions maintained their Divine light and reminded us of our collective responsibilities. They served as our moon and stars reflecting, calling us to our true human nature—equity and justice for all.

When greed and self-interest become ubiquitous in society, the night falls. These selfish motivators overpower our inclination toward social justice. The sunlight is fading, and dusk is approaching. When social and economic oppression has reached an unacceptable level, society cooperatively works to bring about legislative changes, and we see the approach of the dawn.

Today we are a nation divided. Nearly half of our government officials deny legitimate election results. As a result, congressional initiatives that could advance social justice for all have passed in only one Congressional assembly. The saddest of all recent events was when a Congressional leader was removed from her post because she related election results honestly.

Approximately half of our country is speeding toward dusk while the remainder is advancing the dawn. Will greed and selfishness move us away from sunlight toward darkness? Or will the light of Divine inspiration move in the souls of men and women propelling us toward a new dawn? Which way are we going?

15. Equity vs. Equality:
An Example to Consider

In a discussion about justice and fairness in our schools and our communities, we frequently hear the terms "equity" and "equality" used interchangeably. Yet, without a critical understanding of their differences, we assume that Equality in Education and Equity in Education mean the same thing.

Nothing could be further from the truth. Unfortunately, some legislators use these terms to conceal serious discrepancies in the allocation of resources. "So what is the difference?"

We find in the Bible, "To do justice and judgment is more acceptable to the Lord than sacrifice" (Proverbs 21:3), and in the Qur'an, it says, "Deal not unjustly, and ye shall not be dealt with unjustly" (2:279). These verses warn us to treat each other with justice and fairness.

The word "equality" means sameness. For example, equality in education resources would mean that every student receives the same amount of education funding.

On the other hand, "equity" means to be just and fair when dealing with one another. This is the type of justice referred to in the scriptures cited above.

Using our school funding example, this would mean that every student should receive the amount of funding needed for total development.

Unfortunately, all students are not dealt with justly. For example, some schools have more significant financial and professional resources than others. How is this possible when we hear policymakers argue that educational funds are distributed equally?

This can be explained in an example using property taxes as a basis for school funding. Suppose we look at two hypothetical neighborhoods—one with low-income families and the other with upper-income families. Homes in low-income communities cost $50,000 on average, and higher-income homes cost $150,000.

Legislators and policymakers could establish an "equal" property tax rate of 0.1% per $1,000 of home value. The low-income community would contribute $50 per household for their children's education, but the upper-income families would contribute $150 per child to use for school resources.

It could be argued that this represents equality in educational opportunity—every household is taxed at the same rate.

However, it does not result in equity in education because low-income families are still denied the financial resources required for their children to develop to their full human potential. As a result, they will not be equipped to compete with the wealthier youngsters. This disparity in educational resources is further controlled by limiting portions of our citizens' access to equitable housing.

Similar techniques have been used historically to justify inequity in social justice. For example, education for children of America's formerly enslaved population was separate but unequal. At that time, it was not uncommon to find students in white schools receiving new textbooks while pupils of color were forced to use the throwaway books from the white schools.

Also, as women were introduced into America's labor pool, they were paid less than men for doing the same job. There is a proposal before Congress granting equal rights to men and women, but the Equal Rights Amendment to the US Constitution has yet to be passed.

Still, in the face of these legislative gymnastics to perpetuate inequities in our country, progress is being made, albeit slowly. Under pressure from voters, we have had significant changes in our Executive Branch of government.

Perhaps in the not-too-distant future, we will see equity and equality coalesce. Again, change is possible if we work diligently and cooperatively.

16. Patience Yields Success: Lessons from Juneteenth

Blacks assembled in churches across America on the eve of January 1, 1863, awaiting word of their collective freedom. Many, however, never learned of this gateway to a new life until June 19, 1865. On that day, in Galveston Bay, Texas, 2000, Union Troops freed 250,000 enslaved people unaware of the Emancipation Proclamation. These events spawned great lessons in patience for those who had been relegated to a life of servitude.

There is a verse in Scripture that says, "O you who believe! Persevere in patience and constancy; vie in such perseverance; strengthen each other; and fear The Almighty; that you may prosper" (Qur'an 3:200).

After being stripped from their homeland, forced into chattel slavery, and abused physically and mentally, the spirit of the above message from our Creator would have resonated in their souls. But instead, their endurance was rewarded when God-conscious citizens of all races joined together to eliminate man's inhumanity to his fellow man.

Certain aspects of these events can serve as guidance for our nation today. First, when social justice and inequity find their way into our collective experience, divinely inspired people protest within the parameters of democracy and urge change. As more people understand the specific circumstances and can fully appreciate the injustice, a critical mass is achieved, and the collective consciousness is strong enough to bring about legislative adjustments and change.

A Historical View

Historically this simple progression from injustice to protest and finally to legislative change has evidenced itself time and time again. For example, in 1773, dissatisfaction with governance from abroad and protest eventually led to the Declaration of Independence.

Human injustice during the seventeenth, eighteenth, and nineteenth centuries and systematic protest led to the Emancipation Proclamation in 1863.

Inequality in education rooted in a Separate but Equal doctrine followed by protest and legal battles led to the Brown vs. Board of Education decision in 1954. This desegregation Supreme

Court decision was slow-moving to implementation. Nevertheless, it precipitated a protest that resulted in the Civil Rights Act of 1964.

During these periods of history, the efforts of oppressed people were aided by right-minded individuals—people who were honest and just in their human sensitivities. Their patient, cooperative protests precipitated the change.

Today's Challenges

Today we face new challenges: unchecked gun violence, selective police abuse toward people of color, legislation to disenfranchise thousands of voters, and the perpetuation of systemic economic and social partitioning are examples.

In these cases, just as those viewed historically, the solutions are the same: right-minded, honest, and just people of all racial, ethnic, and religious groups associate around social justice themes—educating one another until critical mass is achieved. At this juncture, their numbers force legislative changes for the good of all citizens.

The late Democratic Representative from Georgia, John Lewis, articulated this process as follows: "My philosophy is very simple, when you see something that is not right, not fair, not just, say something! Do something! Get in trouble! Good trouble! Necessary trouble."

A Bright Future

Flying in the face of the social justice movement is the ubiquitous presence of a made-up story that threatens the very fiber of our democracy. A large portion of our population believes that our current national executives have assumed office illegally.

Notwithstanding, the divinely inspired solution is the same. Honest and just people must struggle against the perpetuation of this political poison and patiently educate others until critical mass is achieved. Then, and only then, can we enjoy legislative changes that can potentially enrich the lives of all Americans?

17. As a Man Thinketh: Establishing Social Justice on Truth

In his 1902 book, "As A Man Thinketh," James Allen writes, "A man is literally what he thinks, his character being the complete sum of all his thoughts." This work supports the idea that good thoughts will develop good character in an individual. Such persons are both pleased with themselves and are pleasing to associate with.

On the other hand, internalizing negative thoughts results in undesirable characteristics. For example, if one thinks that most people are dishonest or selfish, these attributes become defining aspects of their life's decisions. Typically, they display characteristics of greed and selfishness with little concern for the well-being of others.

We are what we think, and our society is reflective of the majority consensus of thought.

Controlling Our Thoughts

In the context of today's fast-paced world, sound bites too often form the foundation of our thoughts. A 30-second advertisement or a word or phrase whose meaning is taken out of context stirs a myriad of ideas in our minds. Our challenge is to discern the truth or falsehood in the ideas that are presented to us.

There is a verse in Scripture that says, "Don't you see that The Almighty created the heavens and the earth in Truth?" (Qur'an 14:19). In my mind, this short verse explains our dilemma. Everything in creation (including humans) must obey natural laws—truth. Just as a celestial body that falls from its orbit burns upon entering the earth's atmosphere, so does man destroy himself when he disobeys the laws of nature.

Controlling our minds requires that we be selective in what ideas we allow to form and grow therein.

The above verse suggests that if we nurture honesty and justice in our thought process as we interact, a socially just and equitable society would be the result.

Social Justice is Built on Truth

Considering these ideas in a social justice context, individuals that think honesty, justice, and equitable treatment of others are desirable characteristics are likely to support social justice and equity. At the same time, persons who display characteristics of indifference to others, personal greed, and selfishness would reflect this thinking in their human interactions. Any of these latter perceptions are too often based on untruths.

Most Americans would rapidly assert their support of justice and equity for all, yet, we see so much evidence of social injustice. How is that possible? Consider these examples.

During the 17th and 18th centuries, the prevailing falsehood relegated women primarily to domestic responsibilities. In addition, laws and cultural practices subjugated their status to that of men. These thoughts legitimized their injustice and inequity.

Similarly, the indigenous people of North America were stripped of their land, language, and culture because of a false sense of superiority and desire for domination by those whom Professor Joel Spring referred to as European Invaders.

Still today, social justice is denied to several minority racial, religious, and ethnic communities. It is perpetuated through an elaborate, ubiquitous system of falsehood and untruths, which are embellished to represent and justify the power of some over others. As these negative thoughts invade the private sanctuary of our minds, they control our analysis of understanding.

We are what we think, and our nation is reflective of the majority's thoughts. *Therefore, Social Justice is an elusive goal until the truth becomes the indisputable underpinning of our collective consciousness.*

18. Math Facts from a Historical Perspective: Building Blocks for Success

Seventy years ago, when I was in second grade, students learned multiplication tables through rote memorization. When youngsters mastered these basic facts, they were able to use them in their further study of mathematics.

They used these skills in arithmetic computations, intuitively learned prime factorization, and successfully worked with fractions. The same skills were utilized when solving rational (fractional) algebraic equations; and much later in the study of Calculus.

Blossoming youngsters were rewarded with self-satisfaction at each step in this education process. Each rung of their ladder of learning motivated them to push forward. Many of these pupils' mastery of Math led to professions such as doctors, engineers, scientists, and university professors.

These basic skills are not emphasized in today's education milieu, especially in schools serving socially and economically partitioned youngsters. Of course, some exceptional teachers recognize the value of these skills, but typically, youngsters are not strongly encouraged to master multiplication facts. Predictably many of these students say they "hate Math;" they are less likely to pursue highly scientific and technological occupations. Sadly, when they become parents, they unconsciously discourage their children from aggressively studying in this academic discipline.

Divine growth process

Although we seldom think about it, most developmental processes have a natural progression. There is a spiritual example of natural growth given to us in scripture. In it, we find, "The parable of those who spend their substance in the way of God is that of a grain of corn: it grows seven ears, and each ear has a hundred grains. So God gives manifold increase to whom He pleases: He cares for all and knows everything (Qur'an 2:261).

Intuitively we recognize that planting a seed in fertile soil provided with water and sunlight yields an abundant return. As in the Math example above, we can metaphorically think of this natural process and apply it to other aspects of our lives.

Similar to basic Math skills, there are specific social skills that youngsters are taught to internalize early in their primary education. For example, they are taught to be honest, treat others as they would like to be treated, and do not take things that belong to others. These skills are also building blocks for success.

When properly nurtured, these societal building blocks are internalized and transferred to others resulting in a just and equitable community of people.

What happens if the environment in which these characteristics are developed is lacking and they are not nurtured? In such cases, the results are quite predictable. For example, in the case of corn, without nutrition, water, and sunlight, the plant withers and eventually dies.

In the case of students learning mathematics, if basic building blocks are not developed, youngsters declare their hatred of Math and, without its mastery, limit their academic potential.

Most importantly, without nurturing honesty, justice, and equity in the hearts and minds of youngsters, they mature with identifiable voids in this aspect of their human development. They become self-centered, calloused to the needs of others, and greedy.

We have individuals at both ends of these extremes in America: Some are totally committed to equity and social justice, and others are equally devoted to greed and self-interest. What can be done? How can we strengthen desirable social justice characteristics in our society? In our Math example, the solution would be to provide remediation of basic Math facts and their application.

I submit that the solution to social injustice is similar. Honesty, justice, and equity are Divinely inspired moral attributes, and they are universal. Therefore, recommending these sacred norms, irrespective of our faith, could help us appreciate one another for the sake of the Almighty. Then and only then could we collaboratively initiate legislative actions that could benefit all citizens.

19. Lessons from a Pandemic: Role of Patience in Our Lives

Praise be to God; the horrors of coronavirus are passing behind us. With more than 50% of our adult population vaccinated, our lives are gradually returning to normal. Now is probably a good time to reflect on what we have learned about patience during this crisis.

There is a verse in scripture that says, "Seek God's help with patient perseverance and prayer; it is indeed hard unless you are humble" (Qur'an 2:45). Also, we find another reference to patience which says, "But in all things approving ourselves as the ministers of God, in much patience, in afflictions, in necessities, in distresses" (2 Corinthians 6:4). These two scripture verses remind us of the importance of patiently persevering in the sight of God.

In 2019 most of us were busy living our day-to-day lives: going to work, taking care of family responsibilities, and enjoying our favorite activities with friends and extended family. Then the Almighty permitted coronavirus to touch our lives, and everything changed.

Businesses were closed—we lost our jobs. Children had to stay home from school—arrangements had to be made for child care. The pandemic prevented us from socializing face-to-face with friends. Even our participation in organized worship services had to be reorganized. These were great challenges that we faced.

But we held on to our faith in God. In time, a vaccine was developed and distributed. Businesses reopened, and now our society is slowly returning to normal. In all of this difficulty, perhaps God wants us to learn something that is beneficial.

If we were so busy working that we could not spend much time with our families, this pandemic forced us to take time. If our children lived in our homes, but we didn't really know them, The Almighty gave us time during this pandemic to learn to understand them. If we were preoccupied with meeting and socializing with friends, this, too, was curtailed.

For the past 17 months, families and communities have faced great difficulties. Yet, they were able to overcome their individual and collective challenges by working cooperatively. We may never have known how much we missed visiting our aging parents had not The Almighty created circumstances that made frequent family visits problematic.

Through this pandemic, God has taught us to be more appreciative of what He has blessed us with and to patiently persevere in all of life's challenges. So let us be those that are grateful and encourage everyone that we know to get vaccinated.

20. Medieval Magic:
Relationship between creator and creation

The strength of Medieval scholars during the Golden Age of Islam (8th through the 15th century) appears metaphorically as "magic" in its ability to advance human civilization juxtaposed to the European Dark ages.

Scholars of this period were able to understand scientific knowledge in the context of Divine revelation. These scholars studied creation scientifically, viewed physical phenomena metaphorically, abstracted, and applied what they had learned to other situations.

A physical observation may spark a mathematical or scientific analogy or a human social phenomenon. This intellectual exercise required a thorough knowledge of a specific field of science and a thorough knowledge of Divine revelation.

Although called the Golden Age of Islam, Professor Nuh Aydin of Kenyon College points out, "It was ethnically and religiously highly diverse in which individuals from many backgrounds contributed to scientific knowledge and progress; being a Muslim was not a prerequisite for this contribution."

Three States of Matter

Now, let's examine an example of a physical phenomenon that lends itself to metaphorical abstraction. If we take an ice cube and apply heat, it melts into water. If we continue to apply heat, eventually, the water becomes steam.

This is an example of a scientific principle known as the Three States of Matter: solid, liquid, and gas. If we think of this abstractly, the ice cube could represent our physical existence— our solid bodies. Applying heat brings out our good moral nature.

As a small child, if I misbehaved, my mother applied caring, loving heat to the seat of my pants, and within minutes my good moral nature became visible, correcting my behavior.

When heat is continuously applied to the ice cube that has now melted into water, steam or water vapor rises into the air.

This stage represents the point at which we no longer need an external reminder. Instead, we have internalized the importance of good moral conduct because we know it is pleasing to our Creator.

If we put that ice cube on the ground, it becomes mud (dirty water) when it melts, but as more heat is applied, the water still rises as vapor and leaves dirt behind.

So, it is in our lives. A typical occurrence in our hustle and bustle existence is overindulgence. Excessive preoccupation with food leads to obesity; preoccupation with money leads to greed and self-interest, and preoccupation with power leads to social and economic partitioning of our nation. We can view these maladies as "dirt" in our human environment.

The metaphorical lesson in the stages of matter is simply this: When a man is preoccupied with material things, he is in his solid state. Then, as his moral sensitivities awaken, he recognizes he has a higher responsibility. He changes from solid to liquid. Finally, his Divine nature awakes in him, and his spiritual self-governs his existence—a gaseous state.

This moral awakening and divine inspiration bring out the best in him and exhibit characteristics aligned with those in support of social justice.

A Lesson for Today

As we face a plethora of challenges in our country, the ability to identify and apply the heat of truth to the ubiquitous presence of deeply embedded inaccuracies is essential for our collective progress. In the story of the Golden Age of Islam is a lesson that has application in our quest for social justice today. Let us learn from Creation and apply Divine insight to our national maladies.

21. Striving with His Guidance Toward Social Justice

The challenges that we face can sometimes bring thoughts of hopelessness. From personal difficulties to global warming, man faces a myriad of obstacles that are beyond his control. Yet, in these cases, we know in our hearts that internalized faith is necessary for success in overcoming these difficulties.

Scripture reminds us that man gets only what he works hard to achieve, and The Almighty will reward our efforts (Qur'an 53:39–41). Therefore, no matter what disturbs our peace of mind, we keep our faith and continue patiently persevering. As time passes, we see that Divine intervention has changed the trajectory of our lives. As a result, inner peace washes over us, and we grow closer to our Creator.

When troubled, we try to explain what is disturbing us to our family, friends, or co-workers. Sometimes they, themselves, are the cause of our inner discomfort. Unfortunately, the more we try to explain, the less they seem to understand, thus frustrating our efforts. Only heavenly influence can return us to a state of inner peace.

"Then I looked on all the works that my hands had wrought, and on the labor that I had labored to do: and, behold, all was vanity and vexation of spirit, and there was no profit under the sun" (Ecclesiastes 2:11).

Often more is required than personal diligence. Cooperation with others is essential for the success that we are seeking. So, we pray for Divine intervention and work cooperatively for the betterment of our neighborhood, community, or nation.

Our Creator's light is truth. Ignorance, the absence of Divine guidance, is darkness. In today's world, the ubiquitous presence of falsehood in our national conversation affects our individual lives. Notwithstanding, as we strive to please our Creator, His light shines, and we are rewarded with peace in our hearts.

Humanity constructs artificial partitions to justify the domination of one group over another. Racial and ethnic divisions, economic and social status, and religious affiliation all serve to dilute The Almighty's message to His creatures.

Just as we had to pray for The Almighty's intervention in our personal lives, so too must we seek His assistance in matters of global dimension.

Collectively, we are facing the challenges of social injustice. Just as our personal lives are not independent of The Almighty's omnipotence, neither are our social and political circumstances. Resolving our common disputes bring us closer to Him.

22. Men and Stones: Power that affects our lives

We have a verse in the Qur'an where the Almighty says that we should save ourselves and our families from a fire whose fuel is men and stones (66:6). Theologically, the fire could refer to the hell fire—a place of torment in which wicked people are placed. Metaphorically we can also think of fire as a difficulty that we face every day in our lives.

This stern admonishment is a useful reminder for us today. The word used for men in this verse is an-Naasu. The root of this word, translated as "men," actually refers to all human beings. The word that translates as a stone is al-Hejaaratu, which means; harden, resist, or prohibit access to something.

Since socially acceptable rules govern human interactions, the underlying assumptions that we share in common—hajara (a form of al Hejaartu)—could be viewed as principles that guide our lives.

Now, we can understand this verse as a warning. The Almighty is giving us clear guidance. If we want peace and prosperity in our lives, do not allow ourselves or our families to be influenced by people and ideas that could lead us away from justice and equity in our society. In the context of today's world, this warning is essential.

Greed and selfishness are overpowering human sensitivities, morality, and justice. Democracy is being challenged by authoritarianism. These influences are so powerful in our society that the voice of spiritually guided and right-minded people seems powerless to initiate and sustain meaningful changes for the good of humanity.

The ubiquitous growth of COVID-19-delta infections has brought these challenges into sharp relief. Many parents recognize the health risks as well as the negative aspects of ideologies and principles being delivered through the public-school environment and classroom instruction. Unfortunately, sincere and well-meaning teachers are powerless against the tidal wave of legislative decisions which govern schools.

Time tested solutions

There have been other periods in United States history in which ideologies and selfish practices dictated the direction of public education. In these instances, clergy, parents, and community leaders developed alternative solutions to save their families from a fire whose fuel is men and stones. The development and growth of the Catholic Schools movement is one example. Desiring an education for their youngsters, Catholics successfully organized and established a nationwide school system reflective of their theological perspective.

Segregation of African Americans also led to the establishment of alternative schools. Although modest in resources, many of these education edifices produced great scholars, businessmen, and national leaders. The prevailing view of the inferiority of African Americans was rejected by these oppressed people. Clergy, parents, and community leaders during this period of history were quite effective in saving their offspring from a fire whose fuel is men and stones.

Possible approaches today

COVID-19-safe environments are also being developed today. The all-pervasive spread of the homeschooling movement is yet another example of a segment of our population that has rejected external authority over their children's spiritual and intellectual growth.

Finally, the past year has also opened the portal to yet another viable approach to an ideologically constructive learning environment—the virtual classroom. Although slow in its acceptance because of its forced implementation, it is a viable alternative because fewer human and economic resources are required for curriculum delivery to large numbers of students. As technology advances, virtual classroom platforms will probably become more popular as a medium of instruction.

A shift in our national social justice paradigm requires that we re-acquaint ourselves with the civics of democracy. Our mass ignorance of this discipline is a useful tool of those that advance authoritarianism. If we conscientiously work to save our families from a fire whose fuel is men and stones, our children will be prepared to undertake the challenge of shifting the pendulum of power.

23. The Gift:
Comprehending His Creation

Mathematics is The Almighty's gift to humanity for understanding His Creation. When I discuss this with students, they immediately acknowledge their understanding. "We use math every day to buy stuff; we use it to explain how far and fast we are traveling, and we use it to measure dimensions of things or ingredients in cooking." These are the typical responses that I received.

So, I remind them that Mathematics influences our lifestyle. I challenge their thinking. "What about the design and manufacturing of the things that we buy? What about the design and manufacturing of vehicles, ships, and planes? What about the design and environmental controls in the great edifices that man constructs?"

Now they start to ponder my question more closely. I explain to them that advances in engineering and physical and social sciences are the results of reflective thought.

Social Implications

Applications of mathematic principles are quite discernible in our society. The social implications, however, are not so apparent. Notwithstanding, human guidance is also detectable in mathematical reasoning. Let's examine a simple example.

How can a ship, made of tons of steel, float? It does not sink because of a principle known as buoyancy. When a ship is built, it is slowly lowered into a body of water. As it enters, it displaces a large volume of water. As the weight of the displaced water approaches the weight of the vessel, the ship no longer sinks.

Reflecting on other scripturally historical accounts, the principle of buoyancy can be viewed in a social context. The story of Noah and his son provides insight for this discussion. A ship could metaphorically represent a social organization. Depending upon our area of interest, we could think of it as a family, a community, or even a nation.

In this analysis, we can think of water as the moral fiber which keeps the social organization "afloat." The family, community, or nation functions cooperatively because all of its members agree to honor the rights and responsibilities of others. The social organization exhibits equity and justice for all of its members. Natural moral laws are Divinely inspired and are not subject to individual interpretation in favor of selfish interest.

You recall that Noah's son did not get on board the boat. He felt that he would be safe in some high place—a mountain. A higher elevation suggests that Noah's son sought safety in a position of power in business, government, or some other high position.

We have seen that greed and the desire for political and economic power that individuals in "high places" have, in many cases, overridden considerations of social justice. Noah's son's refusal to participate in a society bound by Divinely inspired moral principles of mercy, equity, and justice for all resulted in his destruction.

When a family, community, or nation is bound together by Divinely inspired moral laws, they successfully navigate the waters of life. But if this natural law is ignored, individual and societal destruction is inevitable.

24. Universal Synergy: ABCs of Creation

Without some method of numeration life, as we know it, would be problematic. Just think about it—survival without money! In an earlier essay, I discussed the importance of learning Math Facts from a Historical Perspective in the development of youngsters. In this essay, I intend to expand upon this theme from a universal point of view.

Our story begins with a verse from Qur'an. "If you would count the favors of The Almighty, never could you be able to count them. Truly! The Almighty is Oft-Forgiving, Most Merciful," (Qur'an 16:18). Quantification of the blessings that we receive from our Creator engages our spiritual consciousness. We grow in faith as we learn to appreciate all that He provides for us.

Similarly, the story of Mathematics begins with the process of numbering—attempting to answer the questions of "How much or how many?" Human society advances as a consequence of the application of mathematic principles.

Our knowledge of using numeric symbols in measurement and counting dates back to about the sixth millennium (BCE). The

Sumerians and Babylonians used symbolic numeration to measure land and conduct agricultural transactions. The use of symbols to represent large quantities was an important development in human progress.

From its use in the enumeration of items for barter and trade, mathematic principles were abstracted and applied to theoretical situations. It was possible to predict outcomes given rudimentary information, apply computational skills, and anticipate results. Measurement of universal consequences was predictable through the application of these skills.

The evolution of this body of knowledge propelled humanity from counting to Calculus to the exploration of creation on a macro scale and from the presence and absence of a binary pulse to computer technology within a microdomain. All of these technological advancements were the consequence of Mathematic's ability to explain creation.

Just as the simple process of numbering objects and counting them has led to enormous technological advances, so too can the acknowledgment and enumeration of Divine intervention propel humanity toward equity and social justice. Acknowledging Divinely inspired insights into our societal norms, values, and ways of understanding, our interdependence on one another enables humanity to advance intellectually and spiritually.

Spiritual Dimension of Mathematics

No doubt, most people would agree on the importance of numbers in their daily life. Yet many find the mastery of this academic discipline quite challenging. As a Math teacher, I have found that far too many youngsters do not know basic math facts. In many of today's classrooms, students are encouraged to use calculators rather than exercise their own mental capabilities to store and readily access frequently needed data.

Similarly, some youngsters have not learned about their relationship with their Creator. Albeit we may see Him through different eyes, His omnipotent presence in our consciousness is essential for total human development. The symbiotic relationship between Mathematics and Spirituality has contributed significantly to human societal advancement.

During the Medieval period, about the 8th through the 15th centuries, scientists understood that human knowledge was inspired by Divine insights. They used mathematical techniques to study creation, understand physical phenomena metaphorically and abstractly, and apply what they had learned to other situations, thus advancing human knowledge.

Physical observations served as a catalyst and sparked mathematical or scientific analogy. This intellectual exercise required both a thorough knowledge of a specific field of science as well as a thoroughly internalized knowledge of Divine revelation.

Admittedly major advances are credited to well-learned scholars. The mutualistic relationship, however, between Mathematics and Spirituality can be appreciated by all; and it begins when youngsters observe creation and master the abstraction of basic math facts.

25. Charity:
Key to Healthy Community Life

Living the hustle and bustle of our daily life, we seldom stop to consider the source of the many blessings that we take for granted. The food that we eat, our wealth, the knowledge that we possess, our physical and mental health, and even our free time are all gifts that we may use for the betterment or detriment of ourselves and others.

There is a verse in Qur'an which asks, "Who is he that will lend to The Almighty a goodly loan so that He may multiply it to him many times?" (2:245). "Oh," we question, "how can I lend anything to the Creator of all things?" Perhaps sharing with others what he has blessed us with can metaphorically be viewed as a loan to The Almighty.

All that He bestows upon us is only entrusted to us by Him. Our health, our wealth, our knowledge, our time, and our influence on the lives of others are all subject to His confirmation.

The above verse suggests that if we are willing to share what He has blessed us with, He will reward our efforts. He will enrich us and bless us more abundantly. Greed, selfishness, and the hoarding of knowledge and material possessions deny us His generous rewards.

Just as the Almighty gives freely to us all, the charity offers us an opportunity to voluntarily show our gratitude to Him. It is not only giving of our material possessions; charity can also take the form of a kind word, a smile, or even holding our tongues from the utterance of an unkind remark. It even encompasses patience and attentively listening to an idea that we may not support. The blessing may be in a new understanding of an issue that leads to overall community health.

Charity is a universal concept. Trees give up their leaves every Autumn, decompose into the soil, and provide nutrients for a new life in the Spring. Parents charitably sacrifice time and resources for the enhancement of the future growth of their children.

We are reminded in 1 Corinthians 13:2, "And though I have the gift of prophecy, and understand all mysteries, and all knowledge; and though I have all faith so that I could remove mountains, and have not charity, I am nothing. "

Our society is persistent in its narrow understanding of this concept. Broadening our perception may drastically improve our community life.

26. Divine Primes:
Patterns in Creation

Understanding Creation and our roles in it is a never-ending challenge. Scientists and theologians have tackled this challenge for centuries, yet a simple explanation is elusive. Nevertheless, there are many signs and much evidence for our consideration.

While preparing a unit on prime numbers for my middle schoolers, it dawned on me that an analogy could be drawn between human development and the Fundamental Theorem of Arithmetic. Simply stated, without mathematical rigor, this theorem says that any whole number greater than one is either a prime or composite number. So let us apply what we know about prime and composite numbers to the human family of man.

All prime numbers are unique in that they can only be represented by two unique factors: the numeral one and the prime itself. For example, the prime number 5 has only two factors, 1 and 5: $1 \times 5 = 5 \times 1 = 5$. In this example, I randomly selected five. Now let us metaphorically think of prime numbers as numerical representations of individuals.

If we consider one (1) as Creation, then 1 time 5 could represent a person's interaction with Creation. This interaction with Creation is true for any prime number.

By contrast, a composite number is represented as the product of prime numbers. Consider for example, 1 x 3 x 5 = 1 x 5 x 3 = 15. In this case, we can think of 1 x 3 x 5 as the marriage of two people, 3 and 5, and their shared lived experiences with Creation, represented by one (1). Their offspring, 15, has characteristics of both parents represented by the prime factors of 3 and 5. This offspring, who is represented by the number 15, has the characteristics of both parents.

The metaphorical person represented by this composite number also interacts with Creation; 1 x 15 = 15 x 1 = 15. They live new experiences, marry and form additional composite numbers. They then marry another person, represented by 14, who had 2 and 7 as parents.

So these two, 15 and 14, have offspring represented by 210 (15 x 14 = 210). So the person represented by 210 has 15 and 14 as parents and 3 and 5, along with 2 and 7 as grandparents, and so on. Similarly, every human being possesses characteristics of their parents and grandparents.

Primes Representing Characteristics

Upon careful reflection, we can think of many characteristics that prime numbers could represent. For example, two could represent yes and no, up and down, odd or even, etc.; five suggests the human five senses, and seven brings the days in a week to our minds. So let us explore one possibility.

Prime number three suggests the idea of stability. Three points determine a plane. A three-legged stool is stable even when placed on an unleveled surface. Traditionally, there have been three states of matter: solids, liquids, and gases. Physicists, however, have recently identified a fourth—plasma.

We can also find stable characteristics in people. For example, some individuals pursue a goal or idea their entire lives and remain steadfast in their initiatives. Whether family, occupational, or otherwise, they work with a specific goal. In this metaphorical discussion, this type of person could be represented as a composite number that is a multiple of the prime number three (3).

Sometimes when teaching, it is necessary to provide students with a means of connecting to the topic under discussion. This is especially true with Mathematics. So, my main purpose for writing this piece was to provide a method of introducing young learners to the concept of prime numbers. I am hopeful that they will also learn to appreciate that all knowledge is connected for us by our Creator, and understanding these relationships is the key to an illuminated and productive life.

27. Reflection:
Geometry of Inner Peace

We are aware of the utility of Mathematics in its physical applications. Business, economics, engineering, and science are well-known areas of use. However, do we ever consider the importance of Mathematics in understanding our human and social development? For example, middle schoolers study Basic Transformations in Geometry but are seldom reminded of their usefulness in understanding their own human development.

Consider an object of a fixed size and shape in space: a book on a table, for example. One could slide the book, without changing its orientation or direction, from one location on the table to another. In Geometry, this is known as a translation.

Alternately one corner of the book could be held in place, and the book could then be rotated around a fixed point. The book remains in the same general location pointing in a different direction. As you would expect, this transformation is called a rotation.

We could also place a mirror beside our book and compare the book to its image in the mirror. This is known as a reflection.

Intuitively the movements of the book—translation, rotation, and reflection—are easy to understand and visualize. But can they provide guidance for us in our human development?

Transformations in Life

Frequently we find ourselves sliding from one situation to another. Yet, our daily activities, interests, associations, and motivations remain the same and result in similar outcomes. We change our location; there are new faces and new places, but our lives remain the same. This can be seen as a translation—moving from place to place without changing our orientation and life's direction.

Sometimes, however, we do recognize that we need to re-group. We make new friends or begin a new activity in our current situation. We may set a new goal for ourselves. At this point, we remain the same person but attempt to change our life's outcome.

So, translations in our lives move us from place to place. But since our individual success is influenced by social, intellectual, and economic orientations, our lives may remain unchanged. We can rotate our direction, try a new business, or further our education. But, if our basic beliefs and values are not redirected, our progress is marginalized.

Power of Reflection

The third basic geometric transformation, reflection, is indeed the most rewarding for human development. There is a verse in Qur'an in which the Almighty tells us, "He has subjected to you, as from Him, all that is in the heavens and on earth: Behold, in that are Signs indeed for those who reflect" (45:13).

Reflection is seeing yourself as others see you—a mirror image of yourself. In the context of the above verse, it suggests that we see ourselves in the sight of the Almighty.

If we have developed unproductive habits and attempt to change our location or begin a new business or program of study, we may not achieve our desired outcomes. Our minds, heart, and human sensitivities must change if we expect to see our efforts yield alternative results.

So, we begin to reflect on our lives. We go into the quiet places in our inner souls and ask hard questions. How have I contributed to the difficulties that I am experiencing? Is my life guided by a desire to participate equitably and justly when interacting with others? Have I come to understand that greed and excessive self-interest prevent me from achieving the success I am striving for?

Making new friends, moving to a different location, or pursuing an occupation adjustment may not be sufficient. Inner peace is achieved when we reflect on our lives: see ourselves as others see us and bring our lives in

28. Reliance on The Almighty: Foundation of Life

We have in scripture several verses that stress the importance of faith as the foundation of our lives. "As surely as time passes, indeed humanity is lost, except for those that urge one another to truth and patience" (Qur'an 103).

We also find, "Yea, a man may say, Thou hast faith, and I have works: show me thy faith without thy works, and I will show thee my faith by my works" (James 2:18).

In an agricultural community such as we have in central Virginia, the ubiquitous presence of faith should be apparent. We prepare our fields and gardens for planting and have faith that God will send rain to ensure our harvest. We breed our animals having faith that The Almighty will nurture the development and growth of a new life. And we get up every morning secure in our faith that our Creator will permit us to experience a productive day.

However, sometimes He permits conditions that postpone our hopes for a positive outcome. For example, periodic droughts, infertility in some animals, and personal illnesses are all circumstances that challenge our faith. But as the above scripture suggests, if we remain patient and continue working toward our good goals, He will reward our efforts.

These examples, related to our individual and family well-being, are easily discernible. However, faith as the foundation of life is not quite as apparent when viewed in a societal context. Sometimes greed and self-interests cloud our judgment.

When facing a natural catastrophe—hurricane, flood, etc. —our intuition kicks in, and we work cooperatively for our common good. Instinctively we know with faith and guidance from The Almighty, our collective efforts will yield success in overcoming individually unsurmountable disasters.

In matters of equitable access and distribution of societal resources, however, faith in our Creator is sometimes less influential than our rigid adherence to traditional beliefs, norms, values, and practices. So we see the excellence in our humanity manifest itself when fighting a fire or saving a child from drowning. But there is some reluctance when we are invited to support an initiative that ushers in an era of equitable access to societal resources.

The aspiration for utopia is not found in amassing material resources. Instead, it originates in the inner self and is predicated on our understanding that faith in the Almighty is the foundation of all human life and success.

29. Inertia: The Force of Ramadan

The study of Physics is fascinating. But unfortunately, because of our traditional, one-dimensional approach to education, we view this scientific discipline without considering its implications for the Social Sciences and human life.

Simply stated, the Law of Inertia posits that an object in motion continues in a straight line at uniform speed unless an external force acts upon it . Alternatively, the same law would apply to an object at rest. In the world of physical phenomena, the resting object continues to rest until it is forced to move, slow down or stop.

Societal Motion

The above observations are intuitive. They can, however, be applied in other situations as well. For example, during the Colonial period in America, women were considered participants in a cult of domesticity—they were expected to remain at home and care for the family. This movement continued uninterrupted until the Women's Suffrage Movement gained momentum.

Eventually, the force of the Suffrage Movement overpowered the cult of domesticity, and society changed.

Gradually women gained legitimacy as full participants in American democracy.

Similarly, a parallel could be drawn between the freedom from the oppression of women and the legislative end of the oppression of enslaved people in the United States. Apartheid in South Africa and its ultimate termination is another example, as well as the exploitation of natural resources by European powers during the period of Colonialism.

In today's democratic vs. authoritarian sensitive world, perpetual movement is also evidenced. Whether one considers the Left vs. Right conflict in U.S. politics, the Israeli vs. Palestinian struggle, or Russia's invasion of Ukraine, the inertia of one movement continues until a force of equal magnitude, and opposite direction acts upon it.

With careful analysis, one should clearly see that human interaction is the common factor in all of these conflicts. The movement, in all cases, was the result of human initiative.

Regardless of the motivating factors, the results were predictable. Man sets his mind to achieve some goal and moves in a direction to achieve it until something intervenes. These initiatives could be for the advancement of human civilization or to achieve some personal goal. In either case, inertia grows, and the effort continues until it is pushed or pulled off course by an external force.

Spiritual Motion

Inertia exists in Creation, and the principle can be abstracted to societal and political situations. If, in societal and political instances, the force behind these examples of inertia is motivated by individuals. Then it would seem to me that inertia toward human excellence and social justice could be directed through individuals' spiritually inspired guidance and development. Individual self-control can lead to social justice inertia, which is the lesson people of faith learn from Fasting.

Ramadan is the month of fasting for Muslims. For these worshipers and those of other Abrahamic Faiths, the primary lesson to be learned is to deny oneself of physical food during a specified period and focus on spiritual growth. This is done to establish a stronger connection between the individual and The Creator.

Denying one self's physical appetites requires great personal discipline. Although hungry and thirsty, the fasting person understands that this sacrifice develops self-discipline and helps one learn to control physical desires in favor of the development of spiritual insights.

Imagine a society where all its members are more conscious of addressing their spiritual development rather than developing perpetual movement toward a social or political position that could potentially oppress others. This would truly be inertia towards social justice for all.

30. Prayer:
The Universal Elixir

"Seek God's help with patient perseverance and prayer: It is indeed hard, except for those who bring a humble spirit" (Qur'an 2:45).

"On the good ground are they, which in an honest and good heart, having heard the word, keep it, and bring forth fruit with patience" (Luke 8:15).

About fifty-five years ago, I sat in a bunker in Vietnam and asked myself, "What prevents these incoming rockets from destroying this bunker and killing all of us?" At that moment, I understood the importance of faith in The Almighty and the importance of prayer. Since that time, I have learned of and seen the ubiquitous rewards of prayer.

Historically there have been many instances of one group of people attempting to oppress the human potential of another. This is apparent in the story of the Holocaust in Germany, Apartheid in South Africa, and chattel slavery in the United States. In each case, the persecutors attempted to rationalize a justification for their oppression. In each case, the patient prayers of the abused were answered.

In The Medical Journal of Australia, Jantos and Kiat point out, "Some studies have shown a positive association between prayer and improved health outcomes." This finding is intuitive to the experiences of many readers. Most of us are aware of individuals who have gained improved health through prayer.

Contrasted to those who put their faith in prayer and patient perseverance are those who seek advantages through greed and self-interest. Although a minority, they exert power and authority over others through articulate arguments and rationalizations designed to justify their perceived superiority. They deny the Divine decree of the brotherhood and sisterhood of humanity and man's equality in the sight of the Almighty.

Just as we have seen positive outcomes ending the oppression of one group over another and the benefits of prayer in healing, so too can we initiate prayers for an unbiased society. Imagine what would happen if the majority of us prayed for peace and harmony in our collective lives. Our past has taught us a powerful lesson: Faith in The Almighty, prayer, and working cooperatively toward positive change yields favorable results that benefit all of us.

31: The Wheel:
Moving From The Material to The Spiritual

Beginning around 3,500 BC, the history of the wheel is a fascinating story. Additionally, its circular characteristics, when analyzed mathematically, can also provide an opportunity to gain metaphorical insight into an individual's success in life. This analysis is my focus in this brief narrative.

Writing in The Smithsonian Magazine, Megan Gambino points out that the wheel was probably first used as a potter's wheel. It later found application in transportation and agriculture. Throughout the centuries, we now find it used in a myriad of physical and symbolic applications. The device is used in Ferris wheels as well as on TV game shows—The Wheel of Fortune, for example. It has found its way into our cultural language to refer to an unneeded additional person as a "third wheel."

Its circular properties were employed early in history to move large, heavy objects. Tree trunks were placed on the ground, and huge stones were moved from one place to another by rolling them over the logs. This property of the wheel requires further analysis.

Let's examine the cross-section of a log. We can identify two useful measures: the distance around the outside—called the circumference—and the distance from the center to the outside edge—called the radius. Now that the characteristics of this geometric shape have been articulated let's examine its metaphorical implications.

Circle of Life

The circumference of a circle is defined as the locus (path) of all points equal distance from a fixed point—it's center. The radius of a circle is the distance from its center to the outside edge—its circumference. Let's now think of these measures metaphorically.

Let us suppose that the center of a circle represents an individual, and the circumference is a measure of that person's success. It can symbolize the path of one's activities, resulting from knowledge and experience.

Viewed as a wheel, each revolution's circumference covers a fixed distance. We can think of this as personally acquired skills propelling an individual through life. Clearly, the larger the wheel, the larger the circumference, and the greater the distance covered with each revolution.

As we acquire more knowledge and experience, our sphere of influence increases—our radius gets longer. This results in a larger circle, representing greater success. A high school student does not have as much knowledge and experience as a teacher; thus, the pupil has a smaller sphere of influence; by comparison, a classroom teacher would have a much shorter radius, resulting in a smaller sphere of influence than an international world leader would have.

Each of us, as children, possesses a small circle of influence that grows as our knowledge and experience mature. We then grow in our responsibilities epitomized in positions of authority in our families, communities, business, government, etc.

In this simple metaphorical analysis, the tendency for one to see themselves as "more deserving" than others challenges the societal need for justice and equity. Without an overarching boundary, greed, and selfishness can result in pride and arrogance. Divine intervention is necessary to hold self-aggrandizement in check.

Divine Design

The wheel metaphor has within it evidence of a Divine Design in that there is a special relationship between the circumference and radius of a circle. There is a number called Pi, which is defined as the ratio of the circumference of a circle to its radius. If we consider any circle—large or small—its circumference divided by its radius always results in a specific value.

Pi has some unique qualities. Unlike rational numbers such as 7, 2/5, or 9.62, it cannot be represented as a unique whole number, a fraction, or a decimal. It is considered an irrational number with a decimal value of 3.14159 and continues to infinity. Using supercomputers, mathematicians have calculated pi through several trillion decimal places.

Perhaps the most fascinating aspect of pi is this: The ratio of the circumference of a circle to its radius is the same whether the circle is very large or very small. If we think of this as Divine intervention in the affairs of man, this mathematical quantity metaphorically illustrates a Divine design in all that we achieve.

If we are wage earners or world leaders, The Creator's hand is integral to our success. Recognition of His Divine presence rewards our lives with success, peace, love, and happiness.

32: Spiritual Boundaries

"Give us help from trouble: for vain is the help of man" (Psalms 60:11). Assisting someone in trouble is characteristic of healthy community life. It is an unselfish act inspired by a spiritually inspired moral consciousness.

Whether the issue at hand is an individual concern or of national consequence, there are those who want to know "what's in it for me" before they are willing to offer support or assistance.

This has been all too clear in recent positions taken by some of our political leaders. Since 2016 many of them have chosen silence rather than dissent.

Fortunately, in The United States of America, this is an exception rather than a rule. Nevertheless, the above verse reminds us of the importance of placing our trust in The Almighty with our personal affairs and national issues.

Facing Challenges

We face challenges in our lives that are outside of our control. We have all had to wait anxiously on a life-changing event — an interpersonal relationship or perhaps a disturbing medical report. Historically, there have also been laws passed that favor a portion of our citizens while oppressing the human potential of others. These types of legislative actions are also outside of our sphere of control.

These are times that we must find strength, be patient, and wait for Divine support. Sometimes things are so overwhelming that we can only find comfort if we ask our Creator for assistance.

The same message is put forth in Qur'an Chapter 110. "When comes the Help of The Almighty, and Victory; And you see people enter His Religion in crowds; Celebrate the praises of your Lord, and pray for His Forgiveness: For He is Oft-Returning (in Grace and Mercy)."

When The Almighty's help comes, He guarantees a victory over difficulty. Once we have received the call that we had been awaiting, for example, we are overjoyed.

Evidence of victory becomes apparent through our close relationships with others. Our good fortune becomes contagious; it puts a smile on the faces of our family and friends. Perhaps the reader will recall the news reports of people dancing and cheering in the streets of several major cities after Donald Trump lost the 2020 election.

When this level of internal peace is achieved, the Scripture then reminds us to celebrate and praise The Almighty. We could not have achieved a successful outcome without His intervention.

The chapter closes by reminding us that He bestows mercy and forgives us time after time.

Often, the decisions that we make are not well thought out and can lead to destructive consequences. This is true in our individual experiences and in our national legislative agendas. Yet The Creator forgives us and turns a bad situation into one that has a potential benefit. We learn from our mistakes.

Larger Challenges

Today there are disturbing matters that are beyond our individual control. We are challenged by racial, ethnic, religious, economic, and social partitioning. Intolerance is punctuated by mass shootings. Our children are dying in school, an edifice thought to be a safe space.

This malaise continues to worsen as our national leaders fight for partisan control. Violence, bigotry, and discrimination run rampant through our communities as we hope desperately for a cure.

Clearly what is needed is Divine intervention. This spiritual guidance can take the form of a spiritual boundary beyond which no individual would pass.

Such a limiting consciousness would serve to check the activities of those on the extreme "right" motivated by greed and self-interest as well as those on the extreme "left" that champion the cause of excessive individualism.

Divine support advocates a middle path: one in which human dignity and social justice are paramount.

33. Our Goal: Purification of the Soul

In our complex society, we are constantly reminded through the ubiquitous presence of advertising that we "need so-and-so." Once we buy it, we are next encouraged to get the "new improved so-and-so." This repeated focus on acquiring material possessions can lead to the incorrect conclusion that success is in the acquisition of "things."

Interestingly, some scripture verses remind us to measure success quite differently. The Almighty calls our attention to the splendor of the sun and moon, visible during daylight and darkness, respectively. He affirms that the majesty found in the firmaments is the same balanced order and proportion found in creation and can also be found in the human soul. The scriptural, deductive logic then asserts that man is successful who purifies his soul and is a failure if he does not (Qur'an 91:1–11).

A similar reminder is found in Psalms 107:8–9; "Oh that men would praise the Lord for His goodness, and for His wonderful works to the children of men! For He satisfieth the longing soul and filleth the hungry soul with goodness."

Clearly, in the sight of The Almighty, man's quest for material rather than spiritual success is leading our society to an untenable position. Greed and self-interest undermine the Divine nature of freedom and justice.

Ignoring our Divine purpose for existence, freedom, and justice has come to mean an individual is free to exercise his/her "will" even at someone else's expense. Justice is subservient to freedom and permissible only if it does not interfere with individual freedom.

Throughout history, personal ambitions have thwarted the collective success of families, communities, and nations. Acting as individuals or a small group, those advancing this perspective are responsible for the oppression and social injustices recorded throughout time.

Juxtaposed to this is a community of people of all faiths that have internalized their Divine relationship with The Almighty. They understand that the purification of their souls leads to inner peace and harmonious interaction between themselves and others. This is the Divine measure of success.

Imagine, for example, a society in which resources were equitably accessible. This simple change could result in a better-educated society, and as Thomas Jefferson put it, "An educated citizenry is a vital requisite for our survival as a free people."

34: Gratitude:
The Path to Social Justice

There are in scripture several examples of lives well-lived. These individuals each possessed a specific characteristic that propelled them to internal peace and harmony in their lives. Each, in their unique circumstances, persevered patiently in the face of all types of adversity.

Scripture depicts the lives of Joseph (Yusuf), Jonah (Yunus) and Mary (Mariam), and others as people who, in the face of difficulties, remained steadfast in their worship as they faced personal challenges. They patiently persevered to achieve their righteous goals. In time, The Almighty removed their difficulties and gave them relief. As their lives changed, they acknowledged The Creator's assistance and increased their reverence and devotion to Him (Qur'an 94:1–8).

A similar story could be told with respect to the challenges faced by various people throughout history. Several cultural traditions have narratives of oppression relieved by Divine intervention. Apartheid in South Africa would be an example of an oppressed people who found deliverance by Divine intervention. So too, would be the story of chattel slavery in America.

Oppression cannot exist forever in Divine creation. What happens when affliction is removed, but the recipients are ungrateful to The Almighty? They lose Divine guidance and wander in confusion to and fro.

The Story of America

Faced with religious oppression in Europe, many early settlers to the United States found freedom on this continent. They worked to establish an equitable social order—albeit for white men only.

Clear evidence of this can be seen in reference to The Almighty in our national documents and student textbooks such as "The New England Primer." These people's laws and educational objectives were infused with gratitude for The Creator.

The nation grew and prospered for decades. Then greed and self-interest found fertile soil on the North American continent, and gratitude to our Creator was displaced. Freedom and justice came to mean those in power had the freedom to use their influence to manipulate legislation at the expense of justice and the equity of others.

Self-serving individuals are a minority but speak with such authority that their "alternative truths" are taken as fact. God-conscious people of all faiths must speak loudly to support honesty and truth, thus overshadowing the voices of those who would oppress their fellow citizens.

Naturally, there are many people who appreciate Divine intervention in our social and political order. They are thankful to our Creator and recognize their social responsibilities.

However, as the ungrateful and greedy grow in number, our laws, norms of morality, and public policy are changing. Social injustice is rationalized in support of the thirst for political and economic power.

Today our nation is feeling the effects of man's ingratitude toward his Creator. Some of our legislators are so hungry for power that they are willing to support a documented "Big Lie" and block legislation that has the potential to advance social justice in American society.

Although a minority, ingratitude to The Almighty is growing in our country, and greed and self-interest are gaining momentum. The challenge facing all God-conscious people is to hold fast to Divine guidance after any adversity. We should not let greedy non-God-conscious people determine our future.

Working cooperatively, an interfaith community shall prevail. Scripture reminds us, "If my people who are called by my name humble themselves, and pray and seek my face and turn from their wicked ways, then I will hear from heaven and will forgive their sin and heal their land" (2 Chronicles 7:14).

35. Role of the HBCU:
Knowledge and Leadership in a Partitioned Society

I often joke with my wife and tell her that she graduated from the best high school in our city, and I completed my secondary studies at the worst. She completed her undergraduate education in three and a half years, while I took more than fifteen years to earn a Bachelor's degree.

After secondary school, I attended one of our nation's finest Historically Black Colleges and Universities (HBCU). They admitted my academic deficiencies and provided the remedial instruction I needed.

Admissions Officers at some of these institutions understand that many youngsters of color have been denied equitable access to educational opportunities and need an extended hand to achieve meaningful life goals. This is one immediate advantage of HBCU education.

Unfortunately, our schools systematically place youngsters of color in lower expectation classes than their Caucasian counterparts. They are effectively denied quality education and made to believe it is their fault.

Regrettably, my academic shortcomings were severe, and I was forced to leave the university and enlist in the U.S. Marine Corps. During my last tour of duty in Vietnam, I wrote to the university asking to return and continue my studies.

They replied that there was nothing in my previous academic records to indicate that I would succeed if given another opportunity. So, they denied my request—"tough love!"

This was the second lesson that my HBCU experience taught me. If I expected to achieve the academic goals I had set for myself, I had to put forth much more effort.

My mom was present when my Ph.D. was conferred and commented, "You have been going to school for the past forty-nine years. Are you finally finished?" I guess by that time. I had thoroughly internalized the second lesson of my HBCU experience.

From a historical perspective, the third and perhaps the most important aspect of opportunities offered at these institutions is the spiritual development of its students. This single characteristic helps students build a strong self-identity. It develops in them a realization of their social responsibility to their subjugated fellow citizens and energizes them to excel in their chosen profession. I have written on the importance of Spirituality in African American Education previously.

Many graduates of these prestigious institutions have become leaders in business, education, and cultural activities. Recognizing their responsibility to society guided by their faith in the Almighty, they have fought for the human rights of themselves and others and continue in these efforts today.

They have demonstrated perseverance in the face of social and economic partitioning. When their families were abused, and their churches and businesses burned, they steadfastly held securely to the collective values of a democratic society.

Three HBCU Characteristics

Years later, after completing my graduate studies, I taught as an adjunct professor at an HBCU. This was a fulfilling experience because I understood the difficulties that students had to overcome just to attend college.

In my classes, students were as unprepared for post-secondary academics as I had been. Some students excelled in their studies and would probably do well in their chosen profession.

I have learned that both groups could benefit just as I did from the three characteristics mentioned herein. Willingness to help others, work hard to achieve one's goals, and reverence for The Almighty would assist in the development of any student and prepare them to fully participate in advancing our American society.

The road of America's HBCUs has been splattered with potholes. Yet, they continue to serve our nation admirably. The model that they represent is one of patient perseverance and steadfastness in the face of difficulties demonstrating their value to American society. Now it is time to recognize their contribution to our nation and the lessons to be learned from them.

36. Enslavement to Empowerment: A Longitudinal Reading of Black History

Tracing the advancement of African People in America is an arduous process. It is one in which the hand of the Almighty is constantly present. His Divine intervention is difficult to appreciate unless one views the past 400 years in a continuum. From 1619 until today, this entire timeline can be understood as three distinct periods: enslavement. development, and empowerment.

The Almighty tells us that He created us in nations and tribes so that we could get to know one another not so that we could hate each other. (Qur'an 49:13). The story of enslaved people brought to North America is a narrative of an ethnic community that grew from a common experience. Their story is ubiquitously presented in a negative light. The descendants of those who experience it are in denial because it lowers their self-esteem, and those who are the descendants of the perpetrators are appalled by the behavior of their ancestors. I recall one of my undergraduate students remarking, "This history makes me ashamed to be white!"

Although each unique event in this history from 1619 is horrific, viewed longitudinally it is a chronicle of patience, courage, determination, and faith all of which are meritorious human qualities that could serve as examples for all Americans. We find in scripture that The Almighty tells us to "seek His help with patience, perseverance and prayer; it is indeed difficult except for those that are humble. (Qur'an 2:45).

Enslavement

The initial experience of America's enslaved people can be characterized by the efforts of individuals. The experiences in the early 1800s of persons such as Sojourner Truth, Nat Turner, Harriet Tubman, and the Underground Railroad in the 1830s were precursors to the Civil War.

Shortly after the signing of the Emancipation Proclamation, Congress adopted the 13th, 14th, and 15th Amendments to the Constitution. The struggle gained new character. It was no longer individuals fighting an unjust system of oppression. Now the entire nation recognized the societal ills of enslavement. But change was slow and icons of progress came onto the scene. Ida B. Wells, Maggie L. Walker, Booker T. Washington, George Washington Carver, and W. E B DuBois made significant contributions throughout the 1800s.

Development

With the founding of the National Association for the Advancement of Colored People (NAACP) in 1909 came a plethora of activities that enhanced Black self-identity. Marcus Garvey and The Honorable Elijah Muhammad encouraged Black identity and working cooperatively as a community for a better future. The Harlem Renaissance gave value to their culture and with it came ethnic pride. The 1954 Brown vs. Board of Education decision gave new life to the struggle and spawned a significant movement.

Empowerment

"And from among you there should be a party who invite to good and enjoin what is right and forbid the wrong, and these it is that shall be successful." (Qur'an 3:104). In this verse, The Almighty tells us that there will be a group of people who will grow out of the masses, will stand for what is right and correct in His sight, and fight against injustice. A few of the icons of this period would include Dr. Martin Luther King Jr., Malcolm X, and Imam W. Deen Mohammed.

These and many others worked cooperatively to unite masses of people who would stand against injustice. Each in their own way identified and articulated the tensions between Whites and Blacks and offered a solution.

This longitudinal history produces the great men and women of today: Former President Barack Obama, Vice-President Kamala Harris, Congressmen Hakeem Jeffries, Justice Ketanji Brown Jackson, and Former Secretary of State General Colin Powell. They were men, women, Democrats, and Republicans all working for the enhancement of our American lives.

These people did not rise to prominence because they were Black. They became national leaders because they represented the best of our national aspirations.

37. Social Justice Icon:
Dr. Martin Luther King Jr.

In a recent article, Role of the HBCU, I discussed the contributions that graduates of these august institutions have made to American society. One such person is Dr. Martin Luther King, Jr.

His Determination

Born Michael Luther King, Jr., on January 15, 1929, he followed his father and grandfather's academic and professional paths, graduating from Moorehouse College and undertaking a challenging career as a Baptist minister in a racially, economically, and socially partitioned American society.

During the Montgomery, Alabama, bus boycott, which lasted for 382 days, he and his family suffered abuse at the hands of segregationists.

Upon receiving The Nobel Peace Prize in 1964, his thrust for the rights of African Americans was accented by traveling over 6 million miles, suffering 20 arrests, and delivering 2,500 speeches from 1956 to 1968.

Reviewing his life, one is struck by his commitment to equity and social justice for all people. Although recognized as a distinguished Civil Rights leader, his ultimate contributions were more universal in scope. The first of these was patience.

We are aware of the Montgomery Bus Boycott but probably never thought about it lasting for more than a year. Imagine the challenges faced by Dr. King and his supporters who had to manage their lives without public transportation and few personal automobiles to use.

This is an example of the patience and extreme sacrifices that are sometimes necessary to bring about meaningful change in a non-egalitarian society.

In the ubiquitous presence of the "Big Lie," we have similar challenges today. We have to create effective methods to identify and confront the racial, economic, and social partitioning ideas being advanced by selfish and greedy power-seekers, those who craved individual wealth and power at the expense of equity and justice for all.

"I Have a Dream"

On August 28, 1963, Dr. King delivered his now-famous "I Have a Dream" speech. The contents of this oration exemplify his immediate concern for racial equality and imply his awareness of a much larger concern than integration—equity and social justice for all citizens of America.

During this oration, Dr. King directly addresses racism and segregation in our country. He says, "Now is the time to rise from the dark and desolate valley of segregation to the sunlit path of racial justice."

He develops another theme in this speech that speaks to a greater measure of human worth than skin color. He says, "I have a dream that my four little children will one day live in a nation where they will not be judged by the color of their skin but by the content of their character."

He engages his listeners in American ideals, thereby sparking an awareness in their consciousness. "I have a dream that one day this nation will rise and live out the true meaning of its creed—we hold these truths to be self-evident: that all men are created equal."

After identifying the malaise of racism in America and calling one's attention to a more accurate measurement of a man's worth, Dr. King warns our nation of the consequences of continued discriminatory practices. "The whirlwinds of revolt will continue to shake the foundations of our nation until the bright day of justice emerges."

The crescendo of this presentation is his call for social justice. "Now is the time to make justice a reality for all of God's children."

In the shadow of chattel slavery, attempted genocide of Native Americans and forced removal of their children to boarding schools, the forcing of Japanese Americans into concentration camps during WWII, and denial of Asians and Hispanics unfettered access to opportunities of citizenship, Dr. King says, "Now is the time to lift our nation from the quicksands of racial injustice to the solid rock of brotherhood."

Closing this presentation, Dr. King dramatically summarized the urgency for people of all races, faiths, and social-economic statuses to recognize that Social Justice has to be the ultimate goal of Life in America. He said, "When we allow freedom to ring, when we let it ring from every village and every hamlet, from every state and every city, we will be able to speed up that day when all of God's children, black men, and white men, Jews, and Gentiles, Protestants, and Catholics, will be able to join hands and sing in the words of the old Negro spiritual: "Free at last! Free at last! Thank God Almighty, we are free at last!"

Universal Guidance for the Future

Dr. King's efforts to emphasize the all-inclusive aspects of the struggle for human rights became more visible in November of 1967. Recognizing that oppression of human potential transcended race, he announced plans for a Poor People's Campaign. This initiative was designed to petition the government for adequate employment opportunities, unemployment benefits, and education for all citizens, improving disadvantaged Americans' social-economic conditions.

Dr. Martin Luther King, Jr. should be recognized as more than a Civil Rights leader. In addition to identifying and encouraging the elimination of the terrible effects of discrimination, his contributions to American society also serve as a reminder of the need for Social Justice. Now, more than fifty years after his death, his life's work serves as a beacon of light guiding America to a future that can only be imagined.

38. Two Rays from a Single Light: Social Justice Requires Interfaith Understanding

When I was a youngster, I attended an African Methodist Episcopal Church. This institution historically played a significant role in the Underground Railroad and assisted many former slaves in finding their freedom. At that time, my parents taught me to pray The Lord's Prayer. In the segregated circumstances of the 1940s and 1950s, the words contained in this prayer provided hope and comfort for many people worldwide and those within our community of color.

The Lord's Prayer

"Our Father which art in heaven, Hallowed be thy name. Thy kingdom comes. Thy will be done in earth, as it is in heaven. Give us this day our daily bread. And forgive us our debts as we forgive our debtors. And lead us not into temptation, but deliver us from evil: For thine is the kingdom, and the power, and the glory, forever." (Matthew 6:9–13).

Later, after I returned from Vietnam, I converted from Christianity to Islam and became a Muslim. During the early years of my Islamic experience, I, like many others, thought that there was a great divide between the two faiths. But as the years passed, I learned that nothing was further from the truth. As a Muslim, I have learned a prayer with a similar spiritual message. The "Verse of the Throne" is a prayer that is often recited by Muslims worldwide

The Verse of the Throne

It says, "God: There is no god but He, the Living, the Self-subsisting, Eternal. No slumber can seize Him nor sleep. His are all things in the heavens and on earth. Who is there can intercede in His presence except as He permits? He knows what (appears to His creatures) before, after, or behind them. Nor shall they understand any of His knowledge except as He wills. His Throne doth extend over the heavens and the earth, and He feels no fatigue in guarding and preserving them for He is the Most High, the Supreme (in glory)." (Qur'an 2:255).

Reflection

Recently I thought about these two prayers, and I realized that both provide comfort to people of faith. I am sure that other faith groups pray similar prayers which promote the same theme—

The glorification of an Almighty Creator and our total dependence upon Him.

There is only one God; our life experiences cause us to see Him through different eyes! The greedy and selfish among humanity would rather see humanity bickering among themselves rather than unite in support of a Divinely-inspired, morally conscious society.

Both verses begin with praise and glorification of The Almighty. Too many people glorify money and political and racial power instead of our Creator. Predictably, in the quest for material possessions, injustice is frequently rationalized.

Next, the above verses remind the worshiper of The Almighty's ultimate authority over our lives. He alone knows the challenges that we face every day. So, we pray and ask for His protection and guidance. People of Faith know that those who would oppress others for selfish gain can do them no harm other than what the Almighty has already decreed.

Both verses end by calling the worshiper's attention to His relationship with His Creation. "For thine is the kingdom, and the power, and the glory"; and "His Throne doth extend over the heavens and the earth."

Today, our nation is suffering from excessive emphasis on social and economic partitioning. Wouldn't it be wonderful if we could see ourselves as an interfaith community of people? However, that is unlikely to occur as long as those that gain control over our lives successfully convince us that we are all different. Racial, ethnic, religious, and economic partitioning is an enemy of social justice.

The utopian society desired by humanity is predicated upon a Divinely-inspired, moral consciousness. The Lord's Prayer, The Verse of The Throne, and many other similar prayers by people of other faiths convey a single message. They bring to the forefront of our conscious mind a solution to the maladies of economic and social partitioning, which are the precursor of social injustice. These and similar prayers are rays from a single Divine Light.

39. Establishing Utopian America: Significance of Black History Month

In the climate of today's Critical Race Theory debate, it is important to understand and appreciate the contributions of various religious, racial, and ethnic communities underpinning our nation. Too often, these contributions are reduced to preconceived stereotypical views.

In my opinion, the United States can benefit greatly from the pluralistic contributions of its citizens. In recognition of Black History month, I have selected the African American community as our sample population.

Since 1976, starting with Gerald Ford, every president has honored Black History month with a proclamation. On this occasion, he said that this celebration enabled our citizens to "seize the opportunity to honor the too-often neglected accomplishments of Black Americans in every area of endeavor throughout our history."

When Ronald Reagan was elected President, he said, "Understanding the history of Black Americans is a key to understanding the strength of our nation."

Although spoken in the context of the African American experience, these two presidential statements speak to the neglected accomplishments and insights into the strength of our nation to which all racial, ethnic, and religious communities have contributed.

Historical Background

American history is marred by the residual practices and policies of chattel slavery. Notwithstanding, the descendants of those slaves have made substantial contributions to our country.

Facing insurmountable odds, these, our countrymen, have established business and educational institutions and have advanced themselves to the highest civic and political positions in our nation. They are a living testimony to Booker T. Washington's observation "… success is to be measured not so much by the position that one has reached in life as by the obstacles which he has overcome."

These and many other noteworthy achievements should be credited to African American people. We must also remember that similar contributions have benefited America that were made by men and women of other racial, ethnic, and religious groups as well.

Recognizing and acknowledging the contributions of all participants in a multi-racial, multi-ethnic, and multi-religious society is the real strength of our nation, and Black History month brings to the forefront of our minds the talents and opportunities afforded us in its pluralistic composition.

The Threat

In today's Congress of The United States, the residual effects of racial, ethnic, and religious partitioning threaten to undermine our democracy. Motivated by power and greed, "The Big Lie" justifies politicians aligning themselves for selfish gains rather than for the good of the nation—the rich get richer, and the poor suffer.

Although aligning oneself racially provides a sense of solidarity, it is too narrow a focus to address the malaise that faces our nation. In scripture, we have a verse that says, "We created you from a male and female, and made you into nations and tribes, that ye may know each other. Verily the most honored of you in the sight of The Almighty is the most righteous of you." (Qur'an 49:13). This verse suggests that our rightly guided moral conduct is more pleasing to our Creator than our nationalistic associations.

Collective Moral Conscious

Addressing the various underpinning ideologies in our country, social and economic policies and legislative practices cannot achieve equity and social justice for all citizens. What is needed is a collective moral consciousness that transcends racial, ethnic, and religious sensitivities. We should see ourselves answering to a higher authority than our individual "group." Dr. Martin Luther King, Jr. envisioned such a nation. Closing his monumental August 23, 1963 speech, he articulated a model of a Utopian America, which he identified as "freedom."

He said, "When we allow freedom to ring, when we let it ring from every village and every hamlet, from every state and every city, we will be able to speed up that day when all of God's children, black men and white men, Jews, and Gentiles, Protestants, and Catholics, will be able to join hands and sing in the words of the old Negro spiritual: "Free at last! Free at last! Thank God Almighty, we are free at last!"

40. Justice is not blind:
Do unto Others

In the historical account of the wise African sage Luqman, he advised his son to honor and obey his parents. The story then generalizes this theme when he tells his son that nothing, good or evil, is hidden from the Creator, even if it were as tiny as a small mustard seed (Qur'an 31:16).

Those of us who are raising or have raised teenagers have similarly warned our offspring—although, in many instances, it seems our advice is unheeded. This lesson we learned as youngsters stay with us our entire lives and permeate our deeds.

No matter how small the good or evil that we do—for our parents and our interactions with others—the Almighty sees it, and we are rewarded or punished for our deeds.

The same idea is presented in Matthew 7:12, "Therefore all things whatsoever ye would that men should do to you, do ye even so to them: for this is the law and the prophets." It is also expressed in the familiar adage, "Do unto others as you would have them do unto you."

With this normative belief pervading our cultural sensitivities, one would think that this guiding principle, "Do unto others," would be evidenced in our human interactions. In most cases, it is. But there have been instances in which the adage seems to conclude with the idea, "Before they do unto you!"

A smile, a kind word, or even making an effort to understand someone else's point of view is rewarded by The Almighty. Unfortunately, too often, our individual concerns supersede this normative practice, and some human interactions are marred by a harsh words or support for selfish initiatives.

This attitude plays itself out in our larger community. Historical racial, social, and economic partitioning practices attest to its influence in American society. As we approach the end of Black History Month, we only have to reflect on the human struggles, sacrifices, and eventual collective cooperation in America to understand the positive and negative effects of "Doing unto others... ."

The prevailing attitude of our nation was reflected in the 1896 Plessy v. Ferguson Supreme Court decision that upheld racial segregation. The spawning of a national moral consciousness gave rise to the 1954 Brown v. Board of Education Supreme Court decision. It ruled that the separate but equal doctrine established in Plessy v. Ferguson had no place in public education because segregated schools were "inherently unequal:" And this pendulum continues to swing toward justice for all.

So, each of us, in our own experiences, has benefited from positive interactions. Just as we try to instill ideals into the moral fiber of our youth, we must continue to practice them ourselves.

The most recent results of positive interactions are the nomination of an African American woman to the Supreme Court of The United States.

Social Justice for all is on the horizon. The Almighty rewards us for all the good that we do by action and intention.

41. Faith! Engendering a Wholesome Life

As the weather warms and the spring flowers and grasses begin to grow, farmers and home gardeners prepare to sow the seed and plant new fruits, vegetables, and flowers to enjoy later in the year. Repeated annually, the significance of this ritualistic practice can escape our conscious minds.

We do not know if our garden will receive enough water and sunlight to produce abundantly. Yet, we prepare our soil with fertilizer, lime, and compost as though we never doubt a successful yield. We plant our garden having faith that The Almighty will provide a wholesome environment that is most beneficial for agricultural success.

We have a verse in scripture which says, "How can you reject faith in The Almighty?—seeing that you were without life, and He gave you life"; (Qur'an 2:28). Now, these words provide us with "food for thought."

We meet our spouses, get married and start a family. We cannot see our future—be it difficult or easy. Yet we have faith that The Almighty will provide a safe, healthy, and nurturing environment for the total growth and development of our marriage and our children.

Life's Challenges

As time passes, life's challenges disturb our inner peace. Sometimes the obstacles are so great that they may seem insurmountable. These are times that we must remember that faith is the foundation of life; "For we walk by faith, not by sight" 2 Corinthians 5:7.

When we experience unpleasant circumstances which are perceived as beyond our control—faith helps us to stay the course.

As scenes of violence, injustice, and human oppression play themselves out on our global stage, we have only to cling to our faith and work cooperatively toward social justice for all to fully understand the dynamic dimension of faith.

The passing of time attests to the rewards. Consider, for example, the enslavement of African people or the forced removal of Native American children from their families. In both cases, through faith in The Almighty, the oppressed people were relieved of their burdens.

Similar examples in the global arena would include apartheid in South Africa and years of colonization of developing nations by European powers. Even today, the ugly scenes in Ukraine serve as reminders of man's inhuman treatment of his fellow man.

In the instances cited, one group of people wants to exploit and oppress another for material gain: economic and/or political power. So, we naturally think of oppressed people requiring patient faith.

Faith can also be viewed from an alternate perspective. The concerns of oppressed people are clearly visible, but the oppressors also conceal fear. They are afraid that power relationships may shift if the subjugated population were to rise to power and influence.

Inherent political and societal norms tend to support legislation that codifies existing power and authority. These correlations continue to exist until a critical mass is reached: one in which individuals acknowledge, within the quiet recesses of their mind, heart, and spirit, that faith in our Creator's laws of justice offers the best promise toward social justice for all.

The critical mass concept mentioned here is historically evidenced, for example, at the end of legal human enslavement in America, the end of colonization in developing nations, and the end of apartheid in South Africa.

Just as the farmer plants seeds with faith that The Creator can provide an environment for natural growth and development, so must we face our life's challenges with Faith.

Regardless of how difficult the circumstances are or our lack of ability to see a solution, The Almighty sees all and has power over everything. His omnipotence is enough to guide and protect us. Faith engenders a wholesome life.

42. The Heart of the Matter: Gateway to our minds

We have a tradition that gives us a simple message of guidance. It reminds us that there is a morsel of flesh in our bodies. If it is healthy, then the whole body is clean, but if it is diseased, then the entire body is sick—indeed, this is the heart.

If we ponder this message in the context of human history, its validity peeks through the curtain of our lived experiences. The oppression of human potential has plagued us generation after generation.

Centuries of wars, military occupations, oppression of human potential, the invasion of one superpower of its sovereign neighbor, and man's greedy self-interest have upset the inherent peaceful balance in the Almighty's Creation.

If the sensitivities of our hearts are motivated by selfishness, then there is no space for concern for the well-being of others. When our hearts have defined a specific objective, our minds begin to develop approaches to achieve that goal.

We find this truth expressed in scripture: "For as he thinketh in his heart, so is he." (Proverbs 23:7.) How could one participate in some of the atrocities that we have historically witnessed if the oppressive individuals or governments were in possession of a clean heart? Do they not understand that each soul is responsible for its actions? Apparently not!

"Do those in whose hearts is a disease think that God will not bring to light all their hidden hatred? (Qur'an, 47:29)." Our hearts are the motivators of all human actions. Kindness in our hearts motivates us to treat others with kindness. Distrust in our hearts results in distrust of others which is reflected in our actions. Hatred in our hearts leads us to actions that are expressive of those feelings.

Our hearts engage our minds to analyze situations from a unique perspective. Our minds translate this analysis into actions—whether positive or negative. This heart-mind-action interchange defines us as individuals. For example, it is not too difficult to discern the heart of Mother Teresa or that of Adolph Hitler.

Our history is plagued with examples of the results of insensitive hearts. Thousands of African Americans were lynched between 1619 and today. But the heart of our country is changing. After more than 200 failed attempts to ratify corrective action over the past 120 years, a new mind is developing among us. Congress has recently passed, and President Biden has signed the Emmett till Anti-lynching Act into law.

Just as lynching is now a federal hate crime, so too will clean hearts engage our minds, and stimulate positive, harmonious connections among all people in our multicultural nation.

Each of us is responsible for our actions which are motivated by our thoughts. Our thoughts, in turn, emerge from the sensitivities in our hearts. Social justice for all Americans starts with a pure heart that is congruent with the Divine laws of The Almighty.

Our heart is the gateway to our mind. We must guard it with care.

43. Seasons of Life: A Cool Spring

Summer, fall, winter, and spring: Each of the four seasons of a year has very different characteristics. We also experience changes in our lives which may be viewed in a seasonal metaphorical context. In spring, days become longer; warm rains and rising temperatures return life to dormant vegetation and bring forth new life.

Winter, on the other hand, is characterized by cold temperatures and inactivity. The colder weather challenges us to protect ourselves with indoor activities, coats, hats, gloves, etc.

We can think of our lives as passing through similar seasons. As we engage in daily activities, we experience pleasure, contentment, and peace. Employment is steady. Our family is supportive. We feel safe, secure, and ready to face new opportunities and challenges. Our lives spawn new life and growth, as does the spring season of each year.

Thunderstorms

Suddenly, the bottom drops out of our peaceful existence. Everything seems to go wrong. COVID-19 hits, and we lose our jobs. Loss of income threatens our homes, and our peace is disturbed. Our elected national leaders deny human justice and equity in favor of greed and self-interest. In the global arena, a sovereign government invades its neighbor ruining human life and destroying property.

A snap of cold weather enters our Spring-like existence. We lose loved ones to a global virus. Social injustice becomes more pervasive through confrontational debates by our legislators, and citizens are forced to leave their home country for safety. Depression grabs the oppressed population like a vise grip. Is there a way out? Will summer ever come?

Sunlight

This is the period when we must remember that The Almighty is always in control—even during these difficult intervals. Sometimes, our trials seem so difficult that we cannot focus on our source of spiritual strength. We are reminded in scripture of the power of our Creator.

"His Throne doth extend over the heavens and the earth, and He feeleth no fatigue in guarding and preserving them for He is the Most High, the Supreme (in glory)" (Qur'an 2:255). Also, we find, "How great are His signs! And how mighty are His wonders! His kingdom is an everlasting kingdom, and His dominion is from generation to generation" (Daniel 4:3).

The above verses remind us that nothing happens without His Divine knowledge or permission. So, if He permitted these difficulties for us, perhaps there is something to be gained from experience. Just as a thunderstorm cleans the atmosphere of pollen and pollutants, so too can life's challenges bring us nearer to our spiritual selves, ridding us of "pollutants."

We learned the value of positive human interactions when they were restricted; we saw the inherent injustice in our society when equitable access to human resources was denied.

Cool days in spring may be a precursor to warm days in summer. Let's keep our eyes on the barometer and thermometer poised for change.

44. Greed:
Antithesis of Social Justice

An objective observer might recognize the combatants in today's Social Justice war. On one side are those that favor power and privilege, and on the other those who champion the call for justice and equality for all. This confrontation is not new. Its precedence is a ubiquitous aspect of world history. Let's examine one scholar's thoughts on this topic.

Alexis de Tocqueville astutely recognized that the privileges of the aristocratic class were on the decline. His seminal work, Democracy in America, was published between 1835 and 1840 and was a compilation of his nine-month visit to America. In his view, "a society, properly organized, could hope to retain liberty in a democratic social order."

De Tocqueville studied America's penal system, slavery, and race relations, analyzing the strengths and weaknesses of American Democracy: its potential and its excesses. In his view, a democratic society properly organized could establish justice and equality for all its citizens. Is America such a society?

Although America is organized so that justice and equality are plausible, they have not yet been obtained. I believe the reason for this is that we are losing sight of our founding father's oath: "One Nation Under God."

Are we losing our spiritual guidance? Scripture reminds us, "And now abideth faith, hope, charity, these three; but the greatest of these is charity. (1 Corinthians 13:13). Also, we find in scripture, "And above all things have fervent charity among yourselves: for charity shall cover the multitude of sins." (1 Peter 4:8).

To answer the questions related to our problematic existence, we must first try to identify the root cause of our insistence on social and economic partitioning. Our ability to visualize others' welfare as contributing partners in our overall community well-being are declining. This unhealthy obsession with the notion of one group's superiority that must dominate and control others speaks to our collective reduction in the understanding of the importance of charity.

Nation-wide shootings, attacks on individuals and minority racial/ religious groups, along with unjust discrimination in our judicial system, have forced this question to the forefront of our consciousness.

I believe the root of our American dilemma is the perpetuation of normative ideals of personal greed. Greed is the antithesis of charity. When politicians' personal greed is rewarded, laws that begin the process of social justice and equity for all are aborted. Satisfaction with one's personal desires is more important than the well-being of our collective whole.

We are conditioned never to be satisfied—we want more than our neighbor. Somehow, we are convinced that this preoccupation with material possessions enhances our self-worth.

Citizens are killed, and murderers sometimes go unpunished. Children are slaughtered, and national leaders do little to stem the sources of this terrible human tragedy.

Scammers recognize this social illness and offer "something for nothing," and we believe it. Advertisers employ language such as "you deserve so-and-so," sparking individual greed.

"Verily (the ends) you strive for are diverse. So, he who gives (in charity) and fears God, and (in all sincerity) testifies to the Truth; We will indeed make smooth for him the path to Ease. But he who is a greedy miser and thinks himself self-sufficient, and calls truth a lie, we will indeed make smooth for him the Path to Misery." (Qur'an, 92:8).

Our societal life can improve, but we must harness our excessive preoccupation with personal greed. Our lives depend upon it.

45. In God We Trust: Requirement for Social Justice

We find these words on our dollar bills, but do we really believe them and live by their injunctions? The original congressional legislators believed in this principle and were guided by it. This is evidenced in our pledge of allegiance, "… One nation under God with liberty and justice for all."

Although full participation in our democracy was narrowly restricted to white males, as time passed, The Almighty's hand intervened, and our nation moved toward recognition of all of its citizens.

Over time these sensitivities changed. Some conservative citizens grew extremely restrictive in their interpretations and interactions. They became intolerant; individual differences over-shadowed their commitment to trust in The Almighty's ability to establish a just and equitable society.

Among liberal citizens were those that elevated their own interpretation of truth and reality above that of The Almighty. Their perspective evolved—any behavior that could be rationally justified was acceptable. They trusted their own thinking over Divine guidance.

So today, we are challenged by extremism on the "right" and "left." Both groups argue that The Almighty supports their limited interpretations of truth and justice. Both believe that The Creator needs their help to correct the corruption. Neither has submitted themselves to fully trusting the Almighty's omnipotent ability to correct all injustice.

In Scripture, we find guidance for us in these troubled times. "If The Almighty is your helper, none can overcome you, and if He withdraws His help from you, who is there who can help you after Him? In The Almighty let believers put their trust." (Qur'an 3:160). God alone can keep us on a trajectory toward equity and social justice for all. Also, in Psalms 118:8, we find, "It is better to trust in the LORD than to put confidence in man."

We have so many examples of people that have trusted the Almighty, and He delivered them from persecution. The sons and daughters of enslaved people have successfully climbed to the highest positions in our nation. Once viewed as obedient and subservient to men, women have achieved lofty and influential positions in our society.

Greed and self-interest have distorted our sense of collective responsibility. Consequently, our democratic society is threatened. Our material possessions and influence will not heal our nation. Our future is predicated on trusting the Almighty. We should not doubt His ability to intercede for our collective good.

46. Snatch the cover off:
Truth and justice will prevail

When I was younger, I recall an expression often used in our community: "Snatch the covers off him." It meant that no matter how long a lie is told and regardless of how convincingly it was articulated, in time, the truth of the matter will become apparent to all.

Anyone that has even superficially followed the January 6th Committee Hearings can testify to the truth of this adage. Speaking before House Oversight Committee on February 27, 2019, Michael Cohen, Trump's former attorney, referred to him as follows, "He is a racist, he is a con man, and he is a cheat." He further prophetically predicted the difficulty of removing him from office should he lose the 2020 election.

Today our nation is still deeply divided. Those on either extreme, the "right" or "left," are often unwilling to examine an alternative perspective than their own.

They listen with ears only attuned to supportive points of view.

Predictably we wonder what the outcome of the January 6th insurrection is. Will responsible individuals be held accountable? Will the process of legal accountability lead to further political partitioning of our nation? What can be done to advance the call for equality and justice for all in a society in which human sensitivities are overshadowed by greed and self-interest?

Yet there is hope

To the attentive observer, it would seem that our situation is worsening. However, history tells quite a different story. We have in Scripture a verse that injustice or evil action could be as small as a grain of a mustard seed hidden in a rock or anywhere in the heavens or on earth. The Almighty sees it and will bring it forth; (Qur'an 31:19).

It is amazing that some individuals believe that their inappropriate behavior would go undetected. Nothing could be further from the truth.

Consider authoritarian leaders, people like Adolf Hitler and Benito Mussolini. These people oppressed the human potential of others for their personal ambitions. In time, however, they were removed from the spotlight, and more of an egalitarian society evolved.

Similarly, governments have supported human oppression. Colonization of independent third-world nations, apartheid in South Africa, and global support of the chattel enslavement of Africans are similar examples.

The Almighty points out in the above verse that no human oppression will remain hidden. As mentioned previously, the House's January 6th investigation is clearly "snatching the covers off" a well-planned insurrection effort. So we should not be disheartened—truth and honesty always ring loudest in time.

Therefore, our collective tasks are twofold: first, keep faith that The Omnipotent is always in control, and second, we must work cooperatively toward establishing equity, justice, and harmonious society for all.

47. Advice and Counsel:
If he does not listen, adversity will teach him
(African Proverb)

Have you ever watched a movie in which a vile and evil person destroys the lives or property of others? When they are caught and have to face the consequences of their actions, some beg for forgiveness and mercy. Some even pledge never to commit the same or similar offenses again.

Although movies are somewhat of a contrived set of circumstances, we have also witnessed similar behavior in our daily lives. I cannot help but believe that this plea for mercy is an expression of regret—albeit, in some instances, it may not be.

Entertainers, political, social, and even, in some instances, religious leaders display physical characteristics of regret in their appearance, even if they do not articulate their feelings. They may lose weight, their faces become drawn and wrinkled, and their entire physical expression is one of depression. Their hearts are not at peace.

In our human history, we have witnessed many examples of "man's inhumanity to man." We have recorded incidents such as the massacre of hundreds of men, women, and children of color in Tulsa, Oklahoma. In 1921 Jim Crow laws forced the descendants of enslaved people to establish an economic base in their own Greenwood community. It flourished only to be destroyed by a hateful white mob that left hundreds killed or wounded and thousands homeless.

But now, 100 years later, this human injustice was acknowledged by President Joe Biden during his recent visit to this historical site.

Recently Pope Francis traveled to Canada to apologize for the Church's abusive practices toward Indigenous children. The inhuman treatment by clergy toward these children has destroyed the lives of thousands.

We have also witnessed the subjugation and oppression of women and the exploitation of thousands of people through colonization and apartheid.

There are those that seem to think that they will never have to answer for their actions. They aggressively support policies that create doubt, confusion, and misrepresentation of the truth.

Consequently, many men and women have and still are suffering oppression and social injustice at the hands of others.

America is Changing

Today, social and economic partitioning continues to oppress the human potential of millions of people. But in every case, as time passes, the Almighty intervenes. The purveyors of injustice must repent or face the consequences of their actions.

The conviction and sentencing of Officer Derek Chauvin in the murder of George Floyd, the racially and ethnically mixed participants in national demonstrations to remove Civil War statues, the presence of Senator Mitt Romney in the DC Black Lives Matter demonstration, and the participation of Representative Liz Chaney as Co-chair of the January 6th Committee are all evidence of our society propelling itself toward a brighter future.

Gradually we are awakening to the realization of Divine intervention. Just as we have witnessed historically, truth and justice will prevail.

The Almighty asks us to redirect our priorities. He says, "By no means shall you attain righteousness unless ye give (freely) of that which you love; and whatever you give, of a truth God knows it well." (Qur'an 3:92).

The human injustices mentioned herein are grounded in greed and the desire for power. As man gives up his individual self-interest, our collective economic and social conditions will improve. Social justice is on the horizon.

48. The Abyss of Self Interest

Toward a national morality

Sometimes I enjoy watching old Western movies and TV shows produced in the 1950s. Although inaccurate in their racial depiction of cowboys—(20% to 25% of whom were Black)—the storylines of most of these shows were developed around positive human interactions. After an evening with The Range Rider, Wyatt Earp, or The Rifleman, the viewer has inner peace from experience. In these films, good always conquers evil.

Some of today's movies leave one with a disquieting feeling: when the villain seems to win, and the victim never receives justice. I recognize that this approach is frequently used to encourage viewers to tune in for the next episode of a series, but it still leaves a void in one's inner spirit.

Motion Picture Producer's Code

Between 1930 and 1967, the Motion Picture Industry initiated a self-imposed system of standards. It was designed as a code of conduct for the production of all motion pictures that would not undermine our nation's moral sensitivities. This self-regulated production code was formulated on three basic principles.

The first principle that the self-imposed standard required was that a film produced for the general public should never lower the moral standards of any viewer. The movie viewer should not leave a video showing in which the sympathies of the observer favored evil and wrongdoing, sin, or any criminal behavior.

Although seen primarily from the perspective of the majority culture, the idea of treating others as you would like to be treated with equity and justice for all was an important lesson to be reinforced in public film production.

The second standard permitted producers to portray life situations and circumstances only to the degree required to suggest their impact on the story. Intimate relations were insinuated but never enacted or displayed in the film production. Monogamy was the accepted standard in those films, and bedroom scenes were never integral to the production.

The third aspect of the movie industry's production code was never to ridicule either the legal process or law enforcement.

These individuals and institutions represented the unquestioned authority required for political, social, and economic stability.

Mass media as educators

The cinema industry has expanded: mass media now includes movies, TV shows, social media platforms, and product advertisements. This constant bombardment is really a method of mass education. We have unconsciously internalized what mass media has presented as acceptable societal norms and standards.

Swallowing this hype, we were gradually fed a diet that undermines our divinely inspired spiritual consciousness. We have learned to accept injustice, indecency, immorality, dishonesty, social partitioning, and economic oppression as normal aspects of our culture. Our moral consciousness is now unbounded, and we sink further into an abyss of greed and selfishness.

It does not matter that gun violence is killing our children while the greedy continue to lobby for legislation that prevents common sense gun laws.

External threats to our democracy are a legitimate concern, but so, too, should be our collective responsibility to provide for our own citizens. How can we, in good conscience, send billions of dollars to other countries while thousands of United States citizens, some of whom are veterans, are hungry and un-housed?

How is it possible for a proven lie, racial hatred, and political bigotry to embrace our country to the extent that they threaten to destroy our democracy?

Ratified in 1791, the 1st Amendment to the U.S. Constitution did not negatively affect movie producers' collective determination. Their code established moral boundaries for the industry, and production companies voluntarily complied. They collectively agreed that these guidelines could yield wholesome entertainment without compromising national norms and values. Isn't it time for us, as a nation, to do likewise?

49. Moral Boundaries

Approximately 100 years after its founding, several friends and I actively participated in our local YMCA program. Our "Y" was not a fancy new building with a swimming pool, gymnasium, and ample parking; no. Ours was an old, three-story building located in a major city's minority neighborhood on one of its busiest major thoroughfares.

On Saturday mornings, my friends and I would walk about two miles to participate in their youth activities. At the start of each program, we were always reminded of three important aspects of total human development: body, mind, and spirit. We were taught if we could balance them in our lives, success was guaranteed.

Given the educational, social, and economic depredation of people of color during the 1950s, it was hard for us to imagine any guarantee of success. Nevertheless, we listened.

Our counselors were public school teachers of color who had sometimes overcome tremendous obstacles to graduate from college. During those preteen years, I did not recognize the great wisdom that they were sharing with us.

Lessons well learned

Now that I am in the autumn of life, I have lived long enough to see the merits of their great wisdom. I have met individuals from all over the world who exhibited balance in their physical, mental, and spiritual lives. I have also encountered some that have not.

The most obvious imbalance that I have seen is the ubiquitous tendency today to isolate spirituality from intellectual prowess. It seems that we have arrived at a juncture in which rationalization attempts to justify any/every human behavior. Without the presence of spiritual sensitivity, one can rationalize and reason in support of the racial, social, and economic partitioning that has become so much a part of life in the United States.

Our schools are reflective of this line of thinking in their insistence on the separation of church and state. Recent research suggests that this disregard for religious sensitivities is one reason for the rise of the homeschooling movement.

The "right" vs. "left" battle has resulted in an exponential increase in gun violence. Some legislators set forth elaborate arguments and reasons for not supporting common-sense gun laws while our nation's children die in their classrooms—a place once thought to be a safe zone.

Acknowledgment of a Divine Creator provides us with a just and equitable boundary. Piercing this boundary results in injustice and inequity. We in the United States need to adopt a middle path. Such an initiative would move the pendulum of social justice toward its center swing. This was the message that my friends and I learned so many years ago at the YMCA.

I recently came across a Moroccan proverb that says, "Instruction in youth is like engraving in stone." Those simple lessons learned as children have propelled many men and women of the United States towards a "more perfect union—" albeit, sometimes, in the face of great struggle.

50. Majestic Forest

Beauty in Diversity

I recently came across the following African Proverb: "A family is like a thick forest, often from outside it's dense, when you're inside each tree has its own position." These words started me thinking about my understanding of a beautiful stand of trees in a forest.

Having been raised in a large urban city, I never realized the majesty of a forest. In my neighborhood, our only environmental green was the traffic lights. There were times when our family went to a park in the city for a picnic. Although this was a pleasant outing, these occasions were sparse.

When my wife and I moved our family to a rural community, I began to see this glorious creation in a new light. The parcel of land that we purchased was total woodland. We had to clear it before we could build our home.

The falling of trees revealed to these city dwellers a variety of species found in the woods. As we observed the characteristics of each species, we learned that the beauty of the forest was the common, natural ability of different trees to co-exist—each contributing to the beauty of the whole.

Pine trees were green throughout the year, representing the presence of life even in the dead of a winter storm. Oaks were huge trees losing their leaves in winter. The leaves decomposed over time and provided nutritious fertilizer for the forest.

When harvested, the woods provided utility: the hardwood of hickory was used to make strong axe handles, the heartwood of cedar lined chests for storage, and the decoratively grained woods of a variety of fruit trees were milled into planks for beautiful furniture.

If we consider individuals in a family or community, various characteristics are also apparent. In this setting, we find some people that are always smiling. Their pleasant attitude and positive outlook brighten any gloomy situation. They are the pines in the forest of man.

Unfortunately, we sometimes face internal and external challenges. To survive, a family or community needs "hardwood"—strong-minded, steadfast, and determined individuals to protect us. The strength of these constituents can be physical, emotional, or spiritual. Regardless of the form taken, their strength binds and protects us.

When pondering the works of great thinkers, we are struck by their contributions both during their lives and after their deaths. Just as a fruit tree displays beautiful blossoms which mature into nutritious fruits, so too make the contributions from the interaction of great intellectual thinkers brighten our lives. As fruit trees give up their wood to be used as furniture when they no longer live, so too do intellectual icons share their accumulated wisdom with us after their deaths.

A forest remains vibrant and healthy as long as the individual species of trees exhibit normal growth. But when blight attacks one species, it not only eliminates itself but the beauty of the forest is compromised, and other trees are eventually affected.

So too, does a family or community grow and prosper as long as its members are healthy. But when blight begins affecting some members, it threatens to destroy the entire community. Our 21st-century blight is the "Big Lie." As it spreads, this menace challenges the future existence of our democracy.

Notwithstanding, there is new growth in the forest. Recent legislation has resulted in positive growth for our community of citizens. Icons of the Confederacy are coming down; there is more apparent racial equity in our government and a unified mass movement against those who block common-sense gun legislation.

Taken as a whole, the forest is still beautiful even with its blight threat. Let's work cooperatively to strengthen and enhance it.

51. God Winks:
Divinely Inspired Success

There is an inspiring poem by Carolyn Joyce Carty entitled "Footprints in the Sand," which succinctly illuminates the presence of The Almighty in our lives. It says that a man saw his life in a dream as footprints on a sandy beach. He understood that two sets of prints represent his walking through life with The Almighty's help and guidance. He observed that through difficult times there was only one set of footprints. So, he asked about this. He was told on those occasions, his Creator was carrying him.

It is the same with all of us. We undertake our daily activities—raising a family, earning a living, and living with others without conscious thought that The Almighty is guiding and protecting us in every situation. Even with His guidance, sometimes life's challenges give us pause.

We may find ourselves in terrible circumstances, having come face to face with a problem that we cannot resolve. It may be a situation requiring knowledge or one requiring financial resources that we do not have. In these times, The Almighty intervenes and provides peace and comfort in our hearts and soul.

Over time, with faith in His Omnipotent Power, our circumstances change.

We are reminded in scripture that "Having therefore obtained help of God, I continue unto this day, witnessing both to small and great" (Act 26:22). Also, we find, "With every difficulty there is relief; Verily, with every difficulty there is relief; So when you are free from your immediate task still labor hard and pray for The Almighty's guidance. (Quran 94:5–9).

Perhaps our most amazing experience is sometimes referred to as a Godwink. These are situations where an unexpected solution to a perplexing problem seems to fall out of the sky. This often occurs when we are least expecting it. Funds needed to improve a personal or family situation suddenly become available to us. Or perhaps we would like to pursue a new educational or business opportunity. Then all of a sudden, there is a crack in the barrier that excludes us, and we get a chance to enter. Our ambitious goal is now possible.

These God Winks occur throughout our lives. The young and uninitiated see them as luck, but the human soul that has become spiritually inspired recognizes these events as divine inspiration.

52. Strength of Purpose:
HBCUs respond to a national need

Recently National Public Radio (NPR) reported that enrollment in Historically Black Colleges and Universities (HBCUs) is on the rise. After a substantial decline since the 1970s, this year's enrollment numbers have significantly increased. This is interesting when one considers the circumstances under which these institutions were established.

In 1937 when the Institute for Colored Youth, now the Cheyney University of Pennsylvania, was founded, the descendants of America's enslaved population faced enormous challenges. Segregation was the law of the land. W.E.B. Dubois called for a "Talented Tenth" to lead America's African American community to economic and social independence. The one hundred or so HBCUs that grew and blossomed from this cesspool of social injustice were reflective of DuBois' observation.

In an earlier essay entitled "Role of the HBCU," I identified three characteristics of these institutions. The first was their empathetic understanding of the challenges faced by students of color. Yet they were willing to admit these youngsters and give them an opportunity to develop their intellect. I myself was one such student.

Tough Love was the second lesson distinguishing the HBCU from traditional institutions of higher education. Regardless of previous circumstances, enrollees were encouraged to take responsibility for their academic success. Academic expectations were established, and excuses were unacceptable. Social and behavioral constraints were enforced. Such guidelines were viewed as a prerequisite for people struggling to achieve full participation in a segregated society.

As it was in the beginning…

One hundred three years ago, the white citizens of Elaine, Arkansas, were enraged by the efforts of Black farmers to unionize. Their anger resulted in the 1919 massacre in which over 200 Blacks were killed. In a 2021 Washington Post article, Gillian Brockell points out that Tulsa was not the only race massacre in United States history. This article identified more than twenty such massacres fueled by avarice and envy of efforts by this group of socially and economically deprived citizens.

The Black Lives Matter movement, spawned by abusive behavior by a few law enforcement officers, echoes similar racial attitudes as those seen in participants in the massacres of Black citizens over the past one hundred years. Coupled with far-right conservatives' legislative agenda, one sees that Jean-Baptiste Alphonse Karr was correct. In 1849 he wrote, "The more things change, the more they stay the same."

Utopia is in collaboration.

I believe that this dark history has contributed to the selection of HBCUs by youngsters of color as their institutions of choice. The future of our nation requires our leaders to collaborate on issues germane to the well-being of our nation. Graduates of HBCUs are keenly aware of societal norms that have contributed to longitudinal injustice. Their balanced perspective is a necessary and important component of our national leadership. Contributions by our newly elected Vice-President and several congressional legislators attest to this conjecture.

Contradictory to the far-right strategy, our nation converges on a unified understanding of equity and social justice. Alexander Hamilton said, "Those who stand for nothing fall for anything.

53. Obesity:
Physical Manifestation of Socioeconomic Malady

In June 2021, the National Center for Health Statistics reported that obesity among Americans was 41.9% of the adult population. This statistic is merely academic until you travel by air and the passenger next to you raises the armrest to accommodate their body mass, imposing on your space.

There are many causes of obesity; excessive caloric intake, media influences, genetics, medications, and stress. Taken in concert, obesity is an abnormal, unhealthy condition.

Now consider "The Fat Cats." These are wealthy, powerful individuals associated with business and politics, many of whom are motivated by greed. Their ambitions can blind them to their societal responsibilities.

In both instances, overindulgence threatens the health and well-being of individuals. In the case of obesity, one's physical life is in danger, juxtaposed to the Fat Cats, who threaten equity and social life within a nation.

54. Education for Social Justice

When a community faces a wildfire, tornado, or hurricane, it is never the case that Whites help only Whites or Blacks help only Blacks. During times of disaster, people help people.

The National Weather Service reported that in August 2005, Hurricane Katrina was responsible for 1,833 fatalities and $108 billion in damages. Everyone pulls together for common dangers like this — their survival depends upon it.

Today we face another national crisis. Hate crimes, mass shootings, and intolerance are on the rise. The marginalization of our citizens into racial, ethnic, and religious partitions is an ongoing threat. Viewed collectively, the damage and number of fatalities from events associated with these human crimes have far exceeded those of Hurricane Katrina.

Our current national leadership is confronting these challenges. We see partitioned minorities appointed to responsible leadership positions in our nation. Although this is a meritorious improvement, there remains the "elephant in the room" — the ubiquitous tendency to see non-Whites as people of less value.

When we hear that a six-year-old boy masterfully plays the concert piano, we say, "Wow, he is only six years old." We are amazed because that is beyond our expectations.

Similarly, we hear on national news, "S/he is the first Black so-and-so or to do such-and-such." This means that this achievement is quite unexpected. The broadcaster is astonished to learn that Blacks have the same human potential as Whites.

Character: The ultimate yardstick

Dr. Martin Luther King, Jr. envisioned a nation where his children would be judged "not by the color of their skin, but by the content of their character." There is evidence that the dream of Dr. King is materializing.

Each of us can identify people that we, at first, thought was undesirable as companions. Later, after we became acquainted with them, we discovered that they possess the same human characteristics, concerns, sensitivities, wants and desires as those whom we consider close friends.

Being a Marine Corps Vietnam veteran, I have seen this firsthand. When people have to depend upon each other, skin color, methods of worship, and cultural barriers are of little consequence.

The future of our nation is predicated upon understanding this truism.

Drop the labels

The combatants for political and economic power vs. those struggling against political and economic oppression attempt to reduce the prevalent issues to categories such as Systemic Racism, White Supremacy, or Critical Race Theory. These explanations place blame rather than offer solutions, and placing blame serves only to deepen distrust and intolerance.

An honest study of United States history is the only viable solution. It is true that people of color were severely oppressed in the United States. It is also true that today's citizens had no part in that dark history. They should not be blamed for it.

It is also true that a yardstick of character is rarely used when evaluating an individual of color in competition for a position of responsibility. This is simply because the employer's experiences do not parallel those of the candidate.

An education that could spawn social justice for all would have certain characteristics. It would be honest, factual, and blameless. It would never be presented either in a way that causes feelings of guilt or in a way that causes feelings of inferiority.

Intolerance, mass shootings, and social violence will not end until we collectively acknowledge the existence of a socioeconomic malaise in the United States. Then, and only then, can a process of education for social justice be effectively implemented, and Dr. Martin Luther King Jr.'s dream can become a reality.

55. Characteristics of Good Teachers

Inspiring Spiritual Boundaries

When I studied Mathematics as an undergraduate student, there was an expression that I have often heard, credited to George Bernard Shaw: "Those that can, do; and those that can't, teach." This assertion conveys a simple idea. People that are highly educated and proficient in their disciplines work in professions that provide suitable rewards for their academic skills. They receive challenging responsibilities, social status, and monetary rewards.

On the other hand, students that are less talented and are unable to compete successfully in our highly competitive society find employment in our nation's classrooms. These supposedly less astute individuals are in fact extremely influential because as a classroom teacher he/she influences the lives of hundreds of students.

In present-day America, teachers hold low professional status. They find themselves challenging disrespectful students, arguing with unappreciative parents, being governed by a rigid hierarchy, and facing possible gun violence. Teaching is a tough job!

Yet, the apparent truism, mentioned above is counter-intuitive and flies in the face (i.e., challenges the character) of dedicated teachers. The Almighty's prophets were teachers and were held in high esteem. Just as they provided foundational spiritual knowledge for individual growth, so too, should classroom teachers provide academic knowledge as well as excellent models of morals and behavior for youngsters.

In today's highly technological society, teachers face a new challenge. These altruistic individuals are asked to prepare students to face a future that they themselves cannot imagine. My third-grade teacher, for example, instilled in me an appreciation for the power of Mathematics in 1952 during the era of black-and-white television. She did not know that her gift of knowledge would be useful in an age of color television, computers, cell phones, and a massive worldwide Internet highway.

So, the classroom teacher should possess several qualities. First, they must have a thorough knowledge of their discipline. University-level teacher certification programs ensure that this requirement is met. They should be empathetic. Students have all types of physical, mental, and emotional challenges to deal with. A successful teacher needs to understand this and provide the necessary support for a student's success.

The third component, which I think is the most important, is that teachers should be spiritually bounded. They should never let their conduct and behavior extend beyond Divinely inspired limits. They understand to advance human society, good vs. evil, right vs wrong, justice vs. injustice, and truth vs. lies cannot be politically motivated or subjectively defined. These social norms must be built upon a Divine platform of human morality.

Teachers in possession of these three characteristics are making a huge contribution to the future of our nation. Their greatest reward is not monetary. It is to hear instead a former student return to their classroom and say, "Thank you." I think Aristotle had it correct when he said, "Those that can, do; those that understand, teach."

56. Coalition for Moral Excellence

A very rare astronomical event occurred in March of 2023. Our moon and five planets, Mercury, Venus, Mars, Jupiter, and Uranus, aligned themselves across the sky in what can be interpreted as an example of cosmic unity. This amazing phenomenon metaphorically speaks to a serious concern: Challenges confronting the ubiquitous practice of maximizing racial, social, and economic partitioning, it seems that The Almighty wants humanity to observe harmony and order in His Creation.

Our societal norm is to emphasize differences and evaluate individual worth based on the group to which they have been assigned. The first level of separation is those who believe in the existence of an Almighty Creator of everything in the universe juxtaposed to non-believers. Although fewer in number, non-believers exert tremendous influence over socially accepted norms, values, and ways of understanding.

Believers are further categorized as: Jews—seen as people of wealth, White Christians--the idealized Americans, Black Christians—emancipated people struggling for equality and social justice, and Muslims—foreigners against whom Christians fought eight Crusades from 1095 to 1291. There are also smaller groups of believers in Buddhism, Native American, and other traditional religions.

Abrahamic Faiths

The majority of Americans identify with one of the Abrahamic faiths: Judaism, Christianity, or Islam. In that Ishmael and Isaac were both sons of Abraham, the followers of these faith groups are of the spiritual descent of brothers. Therefore these believers are spiritual first cousins.

Yet, in our pluralistic society, the tendency is to accentuate differences rather than commonalities. This tendency toward separation moves us away from Abraham's Divine guidance toward a position of domination of one group over another. Scripture reminds us, "And who turns away from the religion of Ibrahim (Abraham) except him who makes himself look foolish? (Qur'an 2:130).

As the alignment of the planets metaphorically suggests, believers are expected to work cooperatively. "The Believers are but a single brotherhood: so make peace and reconciliation between your two (contending) brothers; and fear The Almighty, that ye may receive Mercy." (Qur'an 49:10).

Drawing believers to the importance of cooperating for the advancement of humanity, The Almighty provides further evidence for our reflection. On Sunday, April 9, 2023, those guided by the teachings of Moses, Jesus, and Muhammad (Prayers and Peace be on them) observed Passover, Easter, and Ramadan respectively. Typically occurring every thirty years, this past weekend was the second consecutive year of these spiritual celebrations. Speaking to His prophets, The Almighty says, "Surely your community is one community, and I am your Lord so worship me." (Qur'an 23:52).

The Almighty is One

The ubiquitous tendency toward partitioning is undermining the foundation upon which our nation is built. There is only one Creator: Our unique experiences cause us to view Him through different eyes. If we are unwilling to acknowledge that simple Truth, the struggles for equity and social justice are insurmountable. The achievements of our egalitarian society will be derailed by self-serving initiatives, policies, and legislation.

The Almighty says, "Oh people of scripture! Come to an agreement between us and you: that we shall worship none but God and that we shall ascribe no partner with Him and that none of us shall take others for lords beside God. (Qur'an 3:64).

Our country is plagued by gun violence. Youngsters are dying in our schools yet the majority of our legislators turn a blind eye. The unregulated power of social media is poisoning the minds of young and old alike, and "big tech" rationalizes their position through exercises in sophistry. Our nation is in a morally declining avalanche and legislators are unable to work cooperatively for the health, safety, and well-being of all of its citizens.

When we collectively recognize that our Creator is one, we can then initiate policies, make decisions, and pass legislation that is guided by Divine Law. Human rationalization is too limited. Only a national moral standard, grounded in Divine Laws is able to provide the required spiritual boundary that can propel our nation into the future.

ABOUT THE AUTHOR

Dr. Qadir Abdus-Sabur earned a Bachelor of Science Degree in Mathematics Education from Temple University and worked as a Computer Systems Engineer for twenty-five years. He then continued his studies at The University of Virginia, earning a Doctor of Philosophy Degree in Social Foundations of Education. He taught adjunct classes in Social Foundations of Education and Education Ethics at Virginia Commonwealth University.

He currently serves as Director and Mathematics Teacher at New African Ummah Online School (https://newafricanummah.net), an Internet-based middle school targeting the education of 5th to 8th-grade homeschoolers.

Dr. Qadir also serves as an Imam of the Islamic Center of Prince Edward in Farmville, Virginia, and previously as Resident Imam of Masjid Bilal in Richmond, Virginia. He is also a member of the Board of Directors of Srohume American Alliance, a non-profit corporation with the mission of assisting in establishing schools in Africa.

His recent books are available from amazon.com, and his current thoughts are posted on his blog https://drqadir44.medium.com/.

_____

Made in the USA
Columbia, SC
29 August 2023

22191301R00115